For nearly thirty-five years John C. Parish wrote or taught in the field of American history. From 1922 until his death in 1939 he was a professor of history in the University of California, and, from 1932 to 1936, managing editor of the *Pacific Coast Historical Review*.

One of his chief interests was the history of the West—all of it, from the time when "west" was just over the Alleghenies, to the present. He did not agree with those who held that the westward movement had come to a close about 1890. He questioned "if we have not become so engrossed in the task of writing the obituary of a single frontier—that of settlement—that we have shut our eyes to the fact that the westward movement in its larger sense has been a persistent factor in our national life." He pursued this theme in the essay which now appears in the title position in this volume—an essay that should beget further studies by other scholars in the years to come.

All the essays here presented should serve to stimulate interest in a better understanding of the significance of the American westward movement—of peoples, of institutions, and of ideas.

THE WESTWARD MOVEMENT

The Persistence
of the Westward Movement and
Other Essays

BY JOHN CARL PARISH

With an Introduction by Dan Elbert Clark

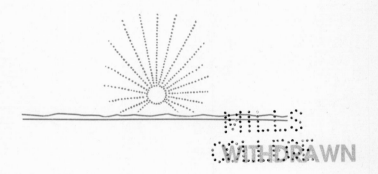

UNIVERSITY OF CALIFORNIA PRESS
BERKELEY AND LOS ANGELES
1943

UNIVERSITY OF CALIFORNIA PRESS
BERKELEY, CALIFORNIA

◇

CAMBRIDGE UNIVERSITY PRESS
LONDON, ENGLAND

PRINTED IN THE UNITED STATES OF AMERICA
BY THE UNIVERSITY OF CALIFORNIA PRESS

This Volume, Among Others Thus Specially Designated, Is
Published in Commemoration of the
SEVENTY-FIFTH ANNIVERSARY
of the Founding of the University of California

PREFACE

·◄ ꝺ·

IT IS CHIEFLY *in the hope of perpetuating John Carl Parish's influence as a historian that these essays of his are brought together and presented in one volume. The force of what he had to say concerning the American westward movement is the stronger for being said all in one place; and the reader is saved the trouble of making search for the various papers, some of which in their first published form are not now easily available. Two of them—one dealing with Edmond Atkin and the other with John Stuart—have not previously been published.*

My own part in the enterprise, though short of being an editorship since the essays needed hardly more than to be assembled, has nevertheless afforded me a welcome opportunity of paying a personal tribute to the memory of Professor Parish. For many years I was closely associated with him in the work and interests of the Department of History on the Los Angeles campus of the University, and in the editorship of the Pacific Historical Review. *In whatever degree my services have been enlisted, they have been given gladly.*

Two of Parish's colleagues, Professor Joseph B. Lockey and Professor Waldemar Westergaard, and his lifelong friend, *Professor Dan Elbert Clark of the University of Oregon, have been called upon for assistance and counsel. The Introduction by Professor Clark, pointing to events and influences in Parish's career, guides the reader toward a just appreciation of his character, his outlook on history, and his contribution to American historiography. Another colleague, Dr. Charles Mowat, has assisted with some slight revision of the paper on John Stuart and has prepared its accompanying notes.*

Mrs. Parish generously consented to assist in the arrangements preliminary to publication. She has also given her permission to print here for the first time the essays not previously published elsewhere.

If the undertaking serves to stimulate interest in a better understanding of the significance of the American westward movement—of peoples, of institutions, and of ideas—it will have justified itself. In any case, it cannot fail to speak for John Carl Parish.

LOUIS KNOTT KOONTZ

Department of History
University of California,
Los Angeles.

ACKNOWLEDGMENTS

FOR PERMISSION to reprint six of the essays in this volume, acknowledgment is made to the several publishers: for "The Persistence of the Westward Movement," to the *Yale Review*, copyright Yale University Press; for "Reflections on the Nature of the Westward Movement," to the Pacific Coast Branch of the American Historical Association; for "The Emergence of the Idea of Manifest Destiny," to the University of California; for "The Intrigues of Doctor James O'Fallon," to the *Mississippi Valley Historical Review;* for "By Sea to California," to the University of Colorado; and for "The West," to the *Dictionary of American History*, published, under the general editorship of James Truslow Adams, by Charles Scribner's Sons.

CONTENTS

———————————·«🙰»·———————————

JOHN CARL PARISH, HISTORIAN

———————————— ·《 》· ————————————

THE ESSAYS and papers which follow were written by a man in whom were combined qualities and
abilities all of which are essential to real achievement
in the profession of historian. He performed his full
share of spadework in the effort to discover the true
facts regarding obscure phases of American history,
and as a researcher he was meticulously scientific; three
of the papers in this volume are illustrative of his contributions of this nature. At the same time, his written
presentation was always characterized by clarity and
readability, and much of his writing is literature. Furthermore, he had gained the experience, knowledge,
and maturity of judgment which, in his later years, enabled him to perform the function of interpreter with
marked success, as is shown in several of the essays here
printed. Finally, he was an inspiring teacher, both of
undergraduates in large classes and of graduate students in small groups or individually.

John C. Parish was born in Des Moines, Iowa, on
July 25, 1881, of parents whose ancestors on both sides
were New Englanders as far back as the early part of

the seventeenth century. He received the degree of
M.Di. in 1902 from the Iowa State Teachers College at
Cedar Falls, where his father was a member of the fac-
ulty. After a short experience as a high school teacher,
he went to the State University of Iowa, from which
institution he received the degrees of Ph.B. in 1905,
M.A. in 1906, and Ph.D. in 1908. As an undergraduate
he was active in student affairs and was the author of
the words of "Old Gold," the alma mater song of the
University. His scholarship is attested by his election to
Phi Beta Kappa. His first historical paper, "The Brib-
ery of Alexander W. McGregor," appeared shortly after
his graduation in 1905 in the *Iowa Journal of History
and Politics*. In October, 1908, he married Ruth Leavitt
Davison of Waterloo, Iowa.

Among Parish's teachers at the University of Iowa
two were most influential in developing the attitudes
and qualities which characterized his later career as a
writer and teacher of history. The first was Benjamin
F. Shambaugh, head of the department of political science and superintendent of the State Historical Society
of Iowa, whose greatest service was his effective direction of research in the field of Iowa history. He im-
pressed indelibly on the minds and consciences of all
who came under his influence the necessity of thorough
research and of painstaking accuracy, of checking and
rechecking every statement and quotation and reference. The other man who in large measure helped to
shape Dr. Parish's methods as a teacher was William

Craig Wilcox, head of the department of history, a competent and helpful critic of the theses and dissertations of his students, a skillful seminar director, and outstanding as a classroom lecturer. Neither Parish nor any other student of Professor Wilcox ever forgot or failed to emulate as far as possible the lucidity, the splendid organization, the sense of humor, and the ability to make history a living subject which Professor Wilcox displayed in his lectures to his classes.

Before completing his graduate work Parish became assistant editor of the publications of the State Historical Society of Iowa. In 1909 he was made associate editor and this position he held until 1910, when he resigned to engage in literary and historical writing in Denver, Colorado. He was professor and head of the department of history at Colorado College from 1914 to 1917. In May of the latter year he entered the officers' training camp at Fort Riley, and for the ensuing two years was in the military service, the last year with the Intelligence Section of the A.E.F. in France, where he attained the rank of captain. After demobilization he returned to Iowa City, and until 1922 was again associate editor of the publications of the State Historical Society. He was the first editor of a new periodical known as *The Palimpsest,* designed to present episodes in Iowa history with complete accuracy but in a literary style that would appeal to the general reader. From 1920 to 1922 he was also lecturer in Iowa history in the State University of Iowa.

In addition to writing several articles, Parish was the author or editor of six books during the period of his early connection with the State Historical Society of Iowa. In 1906 there appeared *The Robert Lucas Journal of the War of 1812,* which threw new light on the ill-fated campaign under General William Hull. This was followed in 1907 by a biography of Robert Lucas, early governor of Ohio and first governor of the Territory of Iowa, inaugurating the Iowa Biographical Series, which has since grown to considerable proportions. He was the author of two other biographies in this series, of John Chambers (1909), second governor of the Territory, and of George Wallace Jones (1911), territorial delegate from Michigan and Wisconsin and one of the first United States senators from Iowa; and he edited *The Autobiography of John Chambers,* published in 1908. His doctoral dissertation, published in 1908, *The Administrative Departments and Offices of Iowa,* was a study which proved of great value when the public archives department was established.

In the biographies, particularly, Parish had opportunity to display the literary qualities that characterized so much of his writing. But it was during the Denver period that he wrote what is in many respects not only his masterpiece, but also an example of good writing which has seldom been surpassed in historical literature. *The Man with the Iron Hand* (published by Houghton Mifflin, 1913) is an account of the early French explorations in the Mississippi Valley, centered about the activities of Henry de Tonty but endeavoring "to place the reader in the position and environment of the native inhabitants in order that he may witness the coming of the whites through the eyes and minds of the Indians." The book was written from original sources and every statement is based on the documents, though the trappings of scholarship are omitted. The style of writing is poles apart from dry-as-dust history. Illustrations of this might be selected almost at random throughout the book. One sentence, which has seemed to the present writer to be especially vivid, will suffice; it comes near the close of the book, after an account of the murder of La Salle and the ruin of his last expedition: "From one end of the valley to the other the white men had traveled; and yet, as the track of a canoe dies out of the water or the shadow of a flying bird passes over the plain and is gone, so now it seemed that the trail of the white men's passing had vanished out of the valley and that the dream that had led to their coming had been lost with the dreamer beneath the waving grass of the Southern plains."

The scene of Dr. Parish's activities shifted from Iowa to California in 1922, when he accepted a position as assistant professor of history at the University of California, Los Angeles. Two years later he was made associate professor, and in 1927 he became a full professor, which position he held at the time of his death on January 13, 1939. He soon became known as one of the University's most stimulating teachers, respected and

beloved by colleagues and students alike for those qualities of mind and spirit which made it impossible for
him ever to be regarded merely as a learned scholar
and gifted mentor. He gave generously of his time and
energies in committee service, and he was especially
helpful in planning and furthering the expansion of
graduate work. He taught in the summer sessions at
the University of California, Berkeley, at Stanford
University, and at the University of Michigan. He was
a visiting scholar at the Huntington Library in 1933–
34 and 1934–35.

Two leaves of absence, in 1925–26 and 1932–33, were
spent in research in France and England. At these
times, and during a previous year, 1908–9, spent in the
archives of France and Spain, he gathered a portion of
his large mass of notes and source materials, which will
ultimately be made available to other students.

All the essays and papers contained in this volume
were writen by Professor Parish while he was at the
University of California, Los Angeles. He was also the
author or editor of numerous other contributions.
Among these were "Jedediah Strong Smith—Path-
finder," in the *Annual Publications* of the Historical
Society of Southern California, XIII, 267–269; "A
Group of Jedediah Strong Smith Documents," in the
same publication, XIII, 304–310; "California through
Four Centuries," which appeared as an introduction to
the Huntington Library *Hand List of California Ex-
hibitions,* 1933; "California Books and Manuscripts in

the Huntington Library," in the *Huntington Library Bulletin,* No. 7; and "A Project for a California Slave Colony in 1851," in the same publication, No. 8. He also wrote articles for the *Dictionary of American Biography* and for the *Dictionary of American History.*

In many respects the most significant monument to the memory of John Carl Parish is the *Pacific Historical Review,* the policies of which he established and directed as its managing editor from its first number in March, 1932, until his resignation in December, 1936. His experience as associate editor for the State Historical Society of Iowa and his active part in the affairs of the Mississippi Valley Historical Association gave him a thorough editorial experience and an awareness of the value of regional historical publications. When he moved to Los Angeles he entered enthusiastically into the activities of the Pacific Coast Branch of the American Historical Association. From the first he was an earnest advocate of a publication that would serve the needs of history and historians in the Pacific area. He was prominent in bringing about the publication of the *Proceedings* of the Branch, the first number of which covered the meeting of 1926.

Five annual numbers were published under the editorship of Professor Parish as chairman of the publication committee. This was regarded as a step in the right direction, but it fell short of the goal of the committee, which from the beginning was a quarterly periodical, as is shown in the minutes of the meeting of

1926. The project was actively discussed at succeeding meetings. In 1928, for instance, a motion was adopted "authorizing this committee to investigate the possibilities of support for the establishment of a Pacific Coast Historical Review and make a report at the next annual meeting." Finally, at the meeting of 1930, after hearing a favorable report from the committee, the members present "voted to authorize the Publication Committee to go ahead and prepare to launch a quarterly in January, 1932." There was general agreement that there was no one so well qualified as Professor Parish to be the managing editor.

The first number of the *Pacific Historical Review* appeared in March, 1932. The first years were years of labor for the editor, who lacked adequate assistance and was under a constant strain of anxiety from the uncertainty of continued financial support. It is clear now that the stress of these years contributed to the illness which led to the passing of John Parish at a time when he should have been at the prime of his powers. That the first editor built wisely and well is attested by the fact that the *Review* is now secure.

The researches and writings of John C. Parish as a productive scholar lie almost entirely in the field of the history of the American West, and he was entitled to be known as an interpreter of the westward movement. Because of this fact it is desirable to indicate his attitude toward the Turner hypothesis. Parish enjoyed the friendship of Professor Turner, of whom he was a

great admirer. He likewise gave his full approval to the
Turner thesis when accepted in accordance with the
meaning of its author. This is indicated in his paper
entitled "Reflections on the Nature of the Westward
Movement," which is printed in the following pages.
"With respect to the importance of our national expansion in its relation, both direct and reactive, to political,
economic, and social life, and in its effect upon American characteristics," he asserts, "no one has gone beyond the vision of Professor Turner a generation ago.
His finely interpretive mind envisaged the whole movement in time and space and quality." He was of the
opinion that later writers had "followed down tempting bypaths without reference to the general map," and
had read meanings into Turner's statements which the
author never intended. At the same time, Parish maintained that historians should not be content to refrain
from constant reëxamination and reappraisal.

Professor Parish himself made one of these reap-
praisals in his very suggestive paper on "The Persistence of the Westward Movement," which, because of its
significance, deserves to supply the title for the present
volume. The basic idea which he elaborates in his paper
is stated in a paragraph near the beginning, after he
has referred to Turner's paper and the general statement that the frontier and the westward movement
came to a close about 1890. "A third of a century has
passed, however, since 1890," he says, "and it seems
pertinent to ask if we have not become so engrossed in

the task of writing the obituary of a single frontier—
that of settlement—that we have shut our eyes to the
fact that the westward movement in its larger sense,
with its succession of many kinds of frontiers followed
by a full sweep of people and their attendant civilization, did not cease in 1890, but has been a persistent
factor in our national life, still tending to distinguish
the American people from the people of European nations." He then proceeds to illustrate and elaborate his
theme by sketching the continued westward movement
of population; of social and political institutions; of
material development in such fields as urbanization,
transportation, production of raw materials, and manufacturing; and of cultural agencies and activities such
as education, public libraries, literary production, the
fine arts, and music. He predicts that long after any
considerable migration of people has ceased "the material and cultural movement will be noticeable."

Numerous other writers in recent years have la-
mented the tendency to accept the implication, no
doubt unjustified, so often drawn from Turner's thesis,
that the importance of the westward movement largely
came to an end in the period around 1890. John C.
Parish, in the paper here printed, was one of the first
to direct attention to the unfortunate results of an acceptance of such a view. A perusal of his many pertinent suggestions may well serve as a stimulus for many
fruitful and illuminating studies by scholars of this
and succeeding generations.

DAN ELBERT CLARK

The Essays

THE PERSISTENCE OF THE
WESTWARD MOVEMENT

—◦◦ ◦ ◦◦—

MANKIND in motion is more interesting than
mankind at rest. Hence explorations, migrations,
and wars have long been the stuff from which the romance of history has been spun. In America, the vigor
with which we moved westward and took possession
of the continent, and the colorful episodes that marked
the process, cast a glamour over this migration that
served for more than a century to hide its true importance. It came to be regarded as an extremely interesting but quite incidental avocation of the American
people, with but little bearing on the real business
of achieving independence, making a constitution, and
developing a nation.

Not until a generation ago did anyone penetrate the
glamour and disclose the real relation of the westward
movement to our national life. In the last three decades,
we have come to realize clearly that the spirit of that
picket line of expansion—the frontier—engendered the
fundamental spirit of the American people and determined the course of events in the nation as a whole.
But, having gained this new vision of the frontier set-

tlement, we have strangely contented ourselves with the assumption that the westward movement ceased to exist at the beginning of the 'nineties, when the more picturesque days were over.

It was in 1893 that Professor Turner published his memorable article on the significance of the frontier in American history. He began by quoting the Superintendent of the Census for 1890 to the effect that the frontier of settlement had vanished; and therefore that the discussion of its extent and shift could no longer have a place in the reports. Then, observing that "this brief official statement marks the closing of a great historic movement," Professor Turner proceeded to point out the importance of the frontier in American life, thus opening up a virgin field for historical research and interpretation. Other scholars followed his lead with studies, intensive and detailed as well as philosophic and interpretative, which furnish us with a distinctly new picture of American development.

A third of a century has passed, however, since 1890, and it seems pertinent to ask if we have not become so engrossed in the task of writing the obituary of a single frontier—that of settlement—that we have shut our eyes to the fact that the westward movement in its larger sense, with its succession of many kinds of frontiers followed by a full sweep of people and their attendant civilization, did not cease in 1890 but has been a persistent factor in our national life, which still tends to distinguish the American people from the people of European nations.

The conquest of the land between the oceans was not achieved solely by the advance of that thin line of pioneers who pushed up river valleys and through mountain gaps into the heart of the continent, and then, not content with this land of promise, fought their way across wearying plains and almost impassable mountains to the western sea. Essential and picturesque and magnificent was the advance of this first line of vigorous humanity, but it must needs be followed by a heavier line, continuing long after the conditions of the frontier had vanished. And with this larger body of people, it was inevitable that new frontiers should pass across the continent—not now the far-flung line of lonely cabin settlers, but the frontiers of material development and transforming ideas. With the pushing westward of these later frontiers and the consolidation of our gains we are now concerned. We are finishing seriously what we began so blithely as our manifest destiny. In the light of these facts, it is well to reappraise the gains made by 1890, and then note the subsequent swing of a movement that is not only persistent but very important in our national life.

The Superintendent of the Census was without doubt justified in announcing as he did the passing of the frontier of settlement, particularly if we accept his definition of the unsettled area as that which had a density of less than two inhabitants to the square mile. Unquestionably one could note, a third of a century ago, the end of an era in American history. Not only had the pioneers thrown their first net of settlement across the continent, but they had pushed to the western coast four lines of transcontinental railway, and had passed a significant milestone of political progress by securing in 1889 and 1890 the admission to the Union of the great block of northwestern States extending from the Dakotas to the Pacific Ocean.

And yet at that time only the first seizure of the land had been achieved. It was at best but a film of population that covered the west half of the continent. Behind the advance line of pioneers, other settlers were coming in answer to the still insistent call of uncrowded regions; and the center of population, though it moved with a more leisurely pace than before, did not cease in 1890 to travel toward the western sea. Between the Atlantic and the Pacific a more adequate network of railroads had to be pushed westward; and there were commonwealths which had yet to complete their evolution from pioneer territorial conditions into statehood.

One could mark, in 1890, frontiers of a new and different sort, advancing into the West, at first tentatively, then with assurance, much as the pioneers had come in earlier years. Some had almost reached the coast, some were lingering in the Mississippi Valley, while others were just pushing across the Appalachians. These were the frontiers of intensive farming, of conservation and reclamation, of adequate banking facilities, of manufacturing industries, of colleges and universities, of political power and influence, of a conventional social system, the frontiers of convenience and comfort and conservatism, of artistic and musical and literary appreciation and production. They were the frontiers that presaged the coming of a highly advanced material civilization, and of a culture of wide significance rather than of merely local importance— a culture changed often by transportation. These frontiers are less tangible than the frontiers of population, and the movements themselves are less easy to trace and are more affected by circumstantial factors. Yet a chronological study of the material and cultural outposts and the general development that supported them indicates clearly that the trend has been steadily westward, directly resulting from the earlier march of peoples.

A consideration of this movement during the last thirty-five years, therefore, involves many phases. The most important element, of course, is the migration of people. Two facts are apparent. One is that there has been a distinct slowing down of the migration into the West. The other is that the movement has nevertheless been persistent, and tremendous in its volume, still continuing (despite the recent rush to Florida) to exceed that in any other direction.

There will always be one fundamental explanation of the movement of mankind, namely, the real or imagined inequality of opportunities in two geographic sections. Just as water seeks a lower level, so humanity is constantly flowing from regions of congestion, of excessive competition, of exhausted resources, or of out-worn attractions, into places where land is cheaper, or opportunities greater, where resources are richer, or life for some reason more alluring. And the current is bound to continue as long as such differences exist.

In the United States the process of reducing these inequalities between sections, however, has gone on apace, as is shown by the decreased rapidity of the west-ward migration during the last third of a century. Once the first, bold, speculative occupation prior to 1890 had been accomplished, once the best free lands had been taken up, the movement passed from its first fevered stage into a second more deliberate stage which per-sists because inequalities still prevail. So far in our his-tory, such differences have presented themselves largely along horizontal lines, and the main movement has been distinctly western, notwithstanding such variants as the migration of farmers northwestward into Can-ada, the trek of negroes northward during and after the late war, and the present considerable march south-ward into Florida.

There is no absolutely accurate speedometer for measuring the movement of peoples. But the most nat-ural method of determining its rapidity and its direc-tion is the location, every ten years, of the center of population. Since 1790 the center of population has steadily marched westward, and curiously enough there has never been a north or south movement sufficiently preponderant to cause this center to vary even as much as a degree north or south of the thirty-ninth parallel. In 1790 it was 23 miles east of Baltimore. In 1890 it was in eastern Indiana, and by 1920 it had gone about 62 miles farther west but was still in the same state. In the century from 1790 to 1890, the average westward movement was 45.8 miles per decade, the greatest progress being 80 miles in the period of the 'fifties. After the year 1890, it progressed less rapidly, the center of population traversing only 14 miles in the next decade. It took on new activity, however, after 1900, shifting in ten years 38.9 miles, a greater distance than in the corresponding first decade of the nineteenth century. In the last decade, the advance has been smaller than in any preceding period, being slightly less than 10 miles.

Ultimately, the center of population will tend to become stabilized as in the older countries of the world, but it is not now possible on the basis of the preceding figures to project a curve ending in the extinction of the westward movement. The increase of people in the United States, coupled with the difference between East and West in the density of population, is bound to prolong the process, and definiteness of prediction is made unwise not only by this fact but also by the uncertainty of such factors as the exhaustion of water supplies or of other natural resources, the discovery of new resources, changes in occupation, the modification of life habits due to the inventive genius of man, and the quantity and quality of immigration from foreign countries.

The connection between this whole subject and immigration is vital. The westward movement has been accelerated and prolonged in the degree that the immigration at eastern ports exceeds that of the western ports (always assuming a balance of immigration over emigration). The vast hordes who have entered our eastern gateways in the last generation, even though they may not have gone far inland, have added to the push which our own colonial forefathers started; and we have come to view their inrush with disquiet, even as the native Indian once saw with increasing alarm the inrush of our ancestors. The later immigrants are themselves a part of the western drive, and they have also been a cause of the westward migration of native-born inhabitants. Hence it may be said of New York City that to the extent that her great increase is recruited from Europe, the growth of the city is, in essence and in effect, as truly a part of the westward movement as the growth of Detroit, Chicago, or Los Angeles.

Incidentally, it should be noted that the large additions by immigration to the population of Pittsburgh, Cleveland, Detroit, and other eastern inland cities, while legitimately constituting a positive factor in the westward movement, have nevertheless had the effect of retarding the westward advance of that imaginary point the center of population, because these accretions represent people who, coming from outside the country, have stopped east of the central point, and so must

be counted as tending to negative the increase of population west of this point. In this respect, the movement of the center of population fails to indicate the
real extent of western migration and partially serves
to hide it.

While immigration in the past third of a century has
thus in the aggregate powerfully stimulated the westward movement, though actually serving as a drag
upon the speedometer, the force of this factor has been
weakened by the great reduction in net immigration
in the years since 1914. If the restrictions upon the
coming of foreigners continue, the advance made by
the center of population during the present decade
will measure much more accurately than in the past the
real extent of migration.

The persistence of the westward swing should have
some reflection in the growth in the West of large urban centers. The following facts may therefore be pertinent. Of the twenty largest cities in the United States
in 1920 only ten have increased more than 100 per
cent in the last three decades. Two of these are east of
the Alleghenies: New York with 124 per cent increase
and Newark with 128 per cent. Six are in the Middle
West: Cleveland with 205 per cent, Detroit with 383
per cent, and Chicago, Milwaukee, Minneapolis, and
Kansas City with from 120 to 150 per cent increase. Two
are in the Far West: Seattle with 636 per cent and Los
Angeles with 1,044 per cent. Although percentages of
increase in young cities may be high while numerical

increase may not be so impressive, this point is somewhat offset by the fact that only the twenty largest cities
of the country have been considered here.

Urban development, however, represents only one
phase of the question. A less striking but more conclu-
sive demonstration of the continuance of the western
trend lies in the fact that every census report since 1890
has shown an increase in the proportion of people west
of the Mississippi River to the total population of the
country. Furthermore, the gain in the West was greater
from 1910 to 1920 than in the decade from 1890 to
1900.

If these observations are sufficient to show that America is still a fluid nation whose people have not ceased
to follow the old routes, let us look next at the natural
sequel of personal migration, namely, the westward
advance of material and cultural frontiers. These may
be said to owe their change of position as much to the
insistence of the West as to any impetus given to them
from the settled East. Their movement was demanded
by the men who had gone on before.

We have assumed that the pioneers went west in
large numbers because of the call of the wild, the desire to get away from the commonplace, conservative
routine of the older civilization. And we read often
that when civilization and conservatism once more trod
upon their heels, they moved on toward the setting sun.
Doubtless this motive, and this tendency toward re-
peated uprooting, did exist. But at the bottom of their

minds the pioneers had other ambitions than the search for a place permanently wild. The individuals were rare who were so desirous of elbow room that they did not look back with longing for at least a few of their fellows and of their old-time comforts. Most of them lived in the hope that the frontier would soon cease to be a frontier. They rushed to the edge of civilization not so much because they loved the hardship, or even the freshness and freedom of life, as because they hoped that by getting to the outer edge before the crowd reached it they would profit when the crowd arrived. Hardships were cheerfully endured for the sake of future advantages. When they were once in position, they craved the coming of at least a portion of the civilization they had left. They agitated for the building of roads from the older settlements. They demanded internal improvements; they pleaded for mail routes and for railroads. They sent back for their neighbors and organized immigration societies. They strove for courts and laws, for statehood, and for participation in political power in the nation. As rapidly as they could, they transformed their new settlements into replicas of their eastern homes. Even those who did move on as neighbors became numerous may have been stirred not so much by the craving for elbow room as by the desire to try again farther west their successful speculation.

It was this attitude toward the civilization they had left behind that brought progress to the national conquest of the continent. Mere pioneering with no attempt at coördination with the East would have been a series of empty gestures. The conditions under which the frontiersmen struggled bred in them a restless energy, a rugged self-reliance, and a tendency to chafe at restraints, but did not extinguish in them the fondness for the older institutions, the inherent Anglo-Saxon tendency to perpetuate traditions. So they drew after them into the West the beginnings of that material development which makes life more comfortable, and, though less rapidly, the elements of that higher civilization which makes life more abundant. These movements, like the advance of population, were composed of the push of a vanguard, followed by a period of consolidation.

By 1890, the movement of material development into the West was in full swing but manifestly incomplete. The frontiers of transportation had already reached the coast, but it still remained to carry westward a more complete network of railroads. Between June 30, 1889, and December 31, 1922, the mileage of railroads in the United States increased about 59 per cent. The increase of mileage east of the Mississippi River during that period was 40 per cent, while the increase west of the river was 80 per cent. At present, railroad construction is at a standstill, partly because the development has caught up with the westward movement of people and industries. Another phase of the question—transportation by means of the automobile—brings us a new manifestation of an old phenomenon. The days of the construction of the Lancaster Pike and the Cumberland Road are reflected in the present efforts to develop great transcontinental roads like the Lincoln, the Coast to Coast, the Santa Fe, and the Custer highways.

Likewise the frontiers of agriculture had reached the Pacific in 1890, but the intensive development of farmland has proceeded more slowly. Since 1890 the centers of production of cotton and of corn have become somewhat stabilized, but the centers of production of wheat, and of oats, and of cereals in general have consistently moved westward, as have the center of the number of farms, the center of improved acreage, and the center of farm values.

The past generation has witnessed notable shifts in the production of raw materials. In 1890 the Great Lakes region led in the lumber industry while the South was successfully rivaling the Northeast for second place. By 1900 the South had surpassed not only the Northeast but the Lakes region as well. In another ten years the Pacific Coast region had risen to second place and was sending lumber to Maine—the old source of our timber supply—and by 1920 the Far West had made tremendous gains upon the lead of the South. The production of oil affords another instance. In 1885 the supply came largely from Pennsylvania and New York. Ohio soon became a strong competitor, and the more recent discoveries of oilfields in Illinois, Kansas, Texas, Oklahoma, and California have transferred the center of production westward by leaps and bounds. Thus the period of western exploration and discovery still lingers with us.

Hand in hand with these phenomena has gone the westward movement of manufactures. The opening of the grainfields in the region beyond the Mississippi resulted in a shift of the flour-milling industry, Minnesota taking and holding the position of first importance. In the five years preceding 1919, Kansas advanced from third to second position in flour production, displacing New York, while Pennsylvania dropped from sixth place to tenth, being dislodged by the western states of Missouri, Washington, Indiana, and Texas.

In the meat-packing industry appears a similar advance. In the same five-year period, Nebraska rose to third in rank in this industry, displacing New York. Ohio displaced Pennsylvania, and Minnesota came up from fourteenth to eighth position. Chicago had long outstripped Cincinnati, but in recent years the most rapid advances have been made by Kansas City, Kansas, and Omaha.

The manufacture of agricultural implements has also had a marked change of base. The recent development of cotton mills in the Carolinas, Georgia, and Alabama, and to a lesser extent in Tennessee and Texas, though primarily a part of the rise of the South, has at the same time been a westward shift challenging the lead of the extreme eastern states of New England.

The whole question of the movement of manufactures may be summed up in the statement that, while

many industries have become localized, the census reports for the last three decades show a steady progress
toward the west of the center of manufacturing in the
United States. In 1920 this point, in spite of the growth
of the automobile industry in Detroit and Cleveland,
had advanced some distance beyond those two cities.

Thus the continuing westward movement of peoples
during the past generation has been accompanied by a
similar movement of material development. As material prosperity has reached the newer communities, the
inhabitants have found themselves with more leisure
and with a growing desire for the refinements of life.
There remains, accordingly, to be noted the more
tardy but no less significant westward swing of the frontiers which may be classed as cultural.

Here we come upon the difficulty of weighing or
measuring a spiritual asset. There is no unit of cultural
progress. The Superintendent of the Census, omnis-
cient though he is, does not attempt to indicate the
center of culture in the United States. He can represent numerically the distribution of railroad lines and
banks and factories, but he cannot locate quantitatively
the permeative influence of good literature, or chart
zones of artistic appreciation, or make graphs of the
diffusion of idealism.

But one who is not limited to the forms of a census
report may at least observe symptoms and symbols of
the spirit. Colleges and libraries, art schools and con-
servatories, public concerts and beautified cities are

indications of its existence. With quality as well as quantity in mind, one may appraise institutions and opportunities and efforts at expression, and arrive at some general conclusions as to the geographical distribution of that intangible thing, culture, and as to the direction of its expansion.

The most obvious and inevitable conclusion is that there has been from the first in America a general diminution of cultural development along an east-to-west line. But the conditions responsible for this diminution are giving way before the westward movement of population and material wealth. High achievements of culture that emerge ahead of time against the background of the West no more invalidate the general principle than does the fact that California was settled before Nebraska invalidate the principle of the westward migration of the American people.

Crossing the Alleghenies in 1890, men passed on into a region where art, painting, and dramatic and musical opportunities increasingly approached the vanishing point. Chicago, although it had at that time just succeeded in crowding Philadelphia out of the second place in population, and was looking forward with enthusiasm to the entertainment of the world at the Fair of 1893, was nevertheless the butt of many jokes because of its crudities. Denver, though it had in a decade trebled its population and passed the 100,000 mark, was hardly more than an overgrown center of a mining region. And on the Pacific Coast, the only real city, San

Francisco, found itself sadly lacking in the cultural advantages of eastern cities of similar size.

There were men among the early pioneers who appreciated the value of higher education, and so there had sprung up the small college, a heritage of the East, and the state university, a historically western and democratic institution. But these institutions became fewer as one traveled west, and even as late as 1890 they were meagerly supported by a people not yet generally affluent, or not yet able to look up from the task of practical conquest of the continent. The Westerner was first engrossed in the struggle against heavy physical odds; later he was obsessed with the need of material establishments. But he did not lose his idealism. And material success, though it tempts individuals and nations into stupid complacence and myopic pride, has nevertheless made its cultural contribution, for it has brought leisure—without which the arts fare badly—and it has brought financial support for unremunerative projects.

Since 1890, there has been a marked westward swing of higher education. The University of Chicago and Stanford University, endowed by western capital, opened their doors in the early 'nineties. The growth of western state universities has been so great that the enrollment numbers are the despair of many who feel that the desire for intellectual culture is so democratic as almost to defeat its own ends. The small colleges with standards rivaling those of their classical prototypes in the East have also increased rapidly since 1890. In this field we can measure progress by recalling that Hall in his *History of Colorado,* published in 1891, remarked of Colorado College: "The work will be in part of a missionary character, amid the Mexicans and Indians who stand at its gates."

That typically eastern organism, the woman's college, is represented in an excellent institution on the Pacific Coast, and those who feel that the West is unredeemable because it still clings to coeducation may take heart from the fact that another college in this region, having acquired a second site (and perhaps a second sight), has laid plans for a segregation of its students on the basis of sex. The extraordinary movement of people into southern California has been the immediate cause of the unique experiment by the University of California of organizing a southern branch, which now after six years' time finds on its campus nearly six thousand students.

Surely educational activity is on the wing westward, and with facilities following numbers the Westerner now sees that the intellectual culture which he used to send his sons east to secure is in a considerable degree available at home. Just so his ancestor in the eastern states once found Harvard, William and Mary, and Yale taking the place of Oxford and Cambridge.

Not soon will the West overtake the East in the development of libraries. Yet there is reason for satisfaction in the growth of the libraries and collections of

Chicago, Madison, St. Louis, and other centers in the Mississippi Valley, followed in more recent years by the establishment on the Pacific Coast of such institutions as the Bancroft Collection at Berkeley, the Hoover War Library at Stanford, and the Henry E. Huntington Library near Los Angeles.

Although there has been a notable activity in historical publication in the Middle West, particularly in connection with state historical societies, the seat of general magazine publication has remained east of the Alleghenies. There are a few promising exceptions, however, which may presage a future expansion. In the meantime, it is increasingly true that eastern magazine editors are taking account of both the readers and the contributors from the West.

As a chapter in the westward advance of culture, the contemporary literature of the Middle West deserves more than a passing mention. It has to do largely with modern conditions in a region that has long been settled, where material prosperity has reached a high state. But it is the literature of a new generation writing in the spirit of the pioneer. It has the vigor and virility of the frontier. It is a revolt. Irksome and unnecessary are the constraints of the older civilization to these writers of the Middle West, and, like the pioneer, they therefore cast them off.

But this is not a new literature any more than the frontier was a new civilization. It is merely another illustration of the fact that culture, when it migrates,

is likely to take on a new form. When the conventions
of the East and the literary spirit of the Middle West
have come together, we shall find that an advance has
been made similar to that which the country has experienced whenever and wherever the vigor and independence of the border have stimulated and enlivened
the older civilization and lost some of their own crudities in the process.

The westward progress of the arts since 1890 is ex-
emplified in the notable musical and artistic growth
of Chicago and in the adornment of her parks and lake
front. It finds expression further on in the establishment of art schools and of coteries of resident artists in
Colorado and New Mexico, and in the support in Denver, for instance, of a beautiful civic center and an unusual system of mountain parks. In the Far West, the
influence of the movement is shown in the growth of
opera and orchestra as well as dramatic and artistic activities in San Francisco and Los Angeles, and in the
emergence of such literary and artistic outposts as La
Jolla, Laguna Beach, and Carmel-by-the-Sea.

Thus during the decades have the frontiers of culture been overtaking the frontiers of settlement and
material growth. These later waves of the westward
movement, these tides of intellectual life—tides for the
most part of conservatism following in the wake of the
more radical element of the early frontier,—have soft-
ened the crudities and harsh vigor of the pioneer. It
rests with the Westerner whether they will lessen his

dynamic energy. If this last phase of the western movement, following one lap behind the frontier of settlement, should bring unchanged to the West the
civilization, the refinements, and the characteristics of
the East, the nation would tend to become homogeneous, and we should lose that element in our life
which has been implied in the old-time spiritual distinction between the East and the West.

But the tendency of culture to change as it migrates,
and the persistent strength of sectionalism in the
United States, will effectually prevent such dull homo-
geneity and will keep our ancient spirit alive. Even
when the last chapter of the westward advance has been
closed and the nation becomes static with reference to
internal movement of people and civilization, we need
not become moribund. France long ago ceased to be a
stage for restless migration and adjustment of people
and ideas. Yet France, like ancient Greece, turned her
activities into the enlargement of an intellectual and
aesthetic horizon. In literature, the arts, and science
she has furnished pioneers of the spirit—frontiersmen
in provinces that have no relation to geography. America, with its superlative material development, and
with an energy ready to be converted to new uses, has
a spiritual call that should preserve it from atrophy.

However, we are concerned here less with the after-
math of the westward movement than with the idea
that for some time to come the phenomenon is likely
to continue. It would, of course, be absurd to maintain

that migration will go on until the population is evenly distributed. Certain geographical facts, if nothing else, would prevent this. Nevertheless, it is evident that the differences between the East and the West are still such that an attraction exists for a large number of people and the preponderating shift is westward. Indeed, long after this migration has ceased, the material and cultural movement will be noticeable.

Finally, it may be well to consider an external phase of the question that has a bearing on the prolongation of this situation. In the United States it has never been a thing unto itself. It has been clearly related to the history of the rest of the world. It began with a westward movement out of Europe—then the undisputed leader in the world's civilization—across the only ocean with which Europe was familiar. Today the world is aware of the presence of another force, the Orient—an ancient civilization awakened into new relationships. As we have been crossing the American continent, there has emerged a new set of problems and possibilities, and the very direction of our growth has brought us up squarely against them.

In 1890 the whole country looked east to New York and Europe. But before a decade had passed, the potential wealth of Alaska was challenging us, and we had reached out into the western ocean and annexed the Hawaiian Islands and acquired possession of the Philippines. Within the next ten years came a great change in the Oriental nations. We found our western and Pacific interests so important that the transcontinental railroads were inadequate, and we built the Panama Canal. The emphasis on these facts is not meant to carry any implication that we shall continue our westward movement beyond the American edge of the Pacific. But it is impossible to escape the conclusion that these new relationships, commercial and otherwise, will continue to increase the importance of the cities of the West which look out upon what Professor Ramsay Traquair calls "the coming Commonwealth of the Pacific."

Today the problems of the Pacific loom so large that an increasing share of the attention of the country is diverted from the Atlantic to the Pacific outlook. Januslike, the nation has come to face in two directions, and it seems inevitable that the persistence of the westward movement within the United States must be affected by the tendency toward an internal distribution and adjustment, not only of people, but also of facilities and ideas, to meet this new dual outlook.

REFLECTIONS ON THE NATURE
OF THE WESTWARD
MOVEMENT

—◄ ❧ ►—

FOR A LONG time in America we have been vitally interested in the things of the West, but perhaps a bit confused by the multitude of words and the array of phrases and facts and ideas about the advance of the pioneer and the conquest of the continent. We have been given all kinds and qualities of interpretations, from the masterly setting forth of the significance of the frontier by Turner to the innumerable attempts to appraise the doings of explorer and miner, town builder and railway promoter, or to present in fiction or essay or humorous extravaganza the local color of life on the outer fringe.

It seems worth while to try to associate these many ideas, and (at the risk of being called a simple soul dealing with obvious facts) to see if there is not a pattern or pertinency that unites them all. Just what are the relations of East and West, fur post and pioneer farm, bad town and camp meeting, vigilance committee and territorial law? Cannot all these and more find their place in a synthesis that will give at least a physical evaluation of that which is most remarkable in American history—namely, the process by which we explored, exploited, occupied, and developed the land between the oceans?

The essence of the process is movement, and the story is dynamic and epic largely because it has to do with mankind in motion rather than in quiescence. We are dealing with a stream of migration that has been coming to the continent for more than three hundred years. Out of this living stream evolved a new nation, and the flow of migration and expansion continued until the farther coast was reached; and since the progress has been so uniformly in one direction we usually express the whole idea in the phrase "the westward movement."

Assuming this, then, to be our general subject of study, let us seek to arrange and appraise the tangible properties of the movement by observing its scope, its direction, and its causation, its setting and its agents, the nature of its elements, and the changing aspects that mark the transition from the earliest days to the present time.

There has been a tendency among some writers to limit the story in point of time, to disregard the colonial period, or at least the period before 1763, as merely an English phenomenon, and to speak of the American frontier as if it had its beginning on the divide of the Appalachians, and as if its relative disappearance about 1890 meant the extinction of the westering tide of expansion. The movement we are observing is something larger than this fragment. It began when the Europeans first came to the shores of the Atlantic, and it is still unfinished although the vanguard of our people long ago reached the Pacific.

The westward advance in the colonial days is of the utmost importance and inseparably a part of the whole. By 1763 men had been pushing west for a hundred and fifty years. In those early decades while the edge of settlement moved inland from the Atlantic toward the Allegheny barrier, the people of the border already presented their characteristic traits and technique. Already the American frontier had been started upon its swing toward the far side of the continent. The men and women of Massachusetts Bay who followed Thomas Hooker through the woods to the inland valley of the Connecticut, and the Virginians who went up the rivers and beyond the Fall Line to find homes in the Piedmont were actors in the same drama with the missionaries and farmers who traveled over the Oregon Trail into the valleys of the Columbia and Willamette, and with the Iowans who later made their more prosaic trek to Long Beach.

The mere change of political control toward the close of the eighteenth century did not mar the continuity of the process. The task, or adventure, was not resigned by one people and taken over by another. A definite racial group began it and their sons and daughters and grandsons and granddaughters carried it on.

Though many who spoke a foreign tongue joined the moving line of humanity, the original stock absorbed them. Thus, to say that there was an English frontier and then an American frontier is to hold to the form and lose the spirit. In the light of retrospection the frontier was always American. The first Englishmen who came were inevitably Americans. Although the truth was long hidden from those who lived on the two shores of the great divorcing ocean, the people who crossed had from the first turned their faces away from their English past and become part and parcel of the American experiment. Destiny, though not yet manifest, was operative two hundred years before it was apparent in the consciousness of its subjects.

If it does violence to the unity of the westward movement to exclude the period of its beginnings, it is just as unnatural to consider the story ended while the migration of people is still keeping up. I have pointed out in another paper[1] the fact that the movement has persisted to the present time despite the passing of the frontier in the later years of the nineteenth century. Thus it is evident that the process fills and animates the entire period of American history.

What shall we say of the scope of the movement geographically? Probably there will be no objection to the statement that the movement we are interested in is that which has brought people and institutions to the present area of the United States. This important fact

[1] For notes see page 45.

follows: there is no portion of the country that has been exempt from the influence of the process, for the edge of the movement has swept over every acre of the national domain and subjected each acre in turn to the experiences and effects of the frontier. Is it surprising that we regard as of the utmost significance in American history that spirited activity which has quickened the life of every generation and permeated the existence of mankind on every spot in the length and breadth of the land?

The West has become a legend in our lives. The direction of our expansion has been so constantly westward that we have almost deified this point of the compass. The phrasemakers have wrought upon our fancies until many have assumed that the way of the westering sun has been a natural migration direction, that "westward ho" is an inspired and universal urge and that westward the course of Empire has always taken its way. But there is nothing sacrosanct about the West. The setting sun leads to no more pots of gold than does the rainbow. The direction of migration in the history of the world has been governed by definite circumstances—largely geographical.

In the great Eurasian land mass the movement was centrifugal—in the direction of India and the Orient as well as toward western Europe and the Atlantic. The occupation of Africa, owing to the Sahara barrier, the wild nature of eastern Africa, and the tardy development of navigation, was postponed to recent times, and,

being thus delayed until the sea was an easy highway,
the movement became not centrifugal but centripetal,
with penetration taking place from all sides toward the
great wild inland. Australia presents some interesting
parallels to our own expansion, but the Russian advance across Siberia is a movement in the precisely op-
posite direction.

In the New World, notwithstanding the fact that explorers and colonists came from the Old World and
went west, the process was not by any means a wholly
westward movement after our coasts had been reached.
South America, like Africa, was settled by a centripetal
penetration. Not yet—after four hundred years—have
the inhabitants quite conquered the distant and difficult interior. It was not so practicable to reach by sea
the farther side of the North American continent.
There remained the alternative of conquest by direct
advance from the east into the interior. But not even
here was the migration universally westward. Cortez,
it is true, captured the city of Mexico and pushed his
way west to the Pacific, but this was merely the preliminary occupation of the tapering bottom of the continent. The real movement of New Spain was northward
from this line of departure which Cortez had established. Within the limits of the present United States,
Spain laid down a far-flung and romantic frontier that
stretched in the course of time from St. Augustine to
northern California. These outposts were not the results of a westward migration. They were thrown out

in a broken line partly from Old Spain, partly in a northern projection from New Spain in defense against the threats of France, England, and Russia.

In the northern part of the continent it was inevitable that France, occupying the mouth of the St. Lawrence, should move westward up the river. But her ambition to reach the western sea dimmed, and when she had crossed half the continent she turned aside and tried to fulfill a quite different purpose. Moving at right angles to the westward axis, she invaded the heart of the continent from the north and from the south as well, and tried to encircle and thwart the English. In this position of advantage she made comparatively little effort to move westward, but devoted her main energies to an eastward movement to control the southern Indian country and the Ohio Valley and meet the English at the crest of the Alleghenies.

In this variegated New World pattern of migration the Anglo-American design is simple, clear, and consistent. Landing on the eastern coast in a zone between two national rivals, the colonists perforce moved west, slowly at first but inexorably. France was removed from the pathway and the advance was more rapid. In the course of time Spain and Mexico alike were crowded to one side, and on the far western coast the American people negotiated their own parent, England, out of Oregon, that they themselves might have a Pacific coast to match their Atlantic, with a broad belt of empire between.

Why is it that people move? Throughout all time migration has kept humanity in a state of flux. Powerful must be the motives that overcome the inertia of a group and send it out on the hard road to strange and often inhospitable lands. There are two sets of impulses which make for change of habitat. One set has to do with conditions within a community, the other with conditions outside. In the first category may be included (1) expulsion from their homeland by an invader or by a hostile faction of their own group, (2) loss of food supply because of drought or extinction of game, (3) major catastrophes such as floods, fires, and epidemics, (4) overcrowding of population—a relative matter depending on the ability of the individual to adapt himself to a diminishing area, and (5) oppression or discipline, which drives out the political or religious dissenter, the fugitive from service or justice or undesired conventions.

All these elements of pressure come from within. The other set of incentives operates from without and includes (1) such practical appeals as newly opened and cheap land, gold strikes, free cattle ranges, closer relation to markets, and better soil and climatic conditions, and (2) less tangible psychological attractions— the lure of the primitive, the call of the unblazed country, unknown and hence mysterious and attractive. There is a potent and compelling influence in the "voice behind the ranges": "something hidden. Go and and find it. . . . Something lost behind the ranges." Not from everyone does this call bring response. In some the instinct of the explorer apparently does not exist. In others it is powerful. This distinction is caught by the stanza from Mary Coleridge:

> We were young, we were merry, we were very, very wise
> And the door stood open at our feast
> When there passed us a woman with the west in her eyes
> And a man with his back to the east.

But after all, whether the pressure comes from within or without, whether the incentive is prosaic or romantic, the motives and explanation of all migrations reduce to one fundamental formula as basic as the fact that water seeks its own level, and that formula is that people move in conformity with the real or fancied difference of advantage between geographical sections. This explains alike the religious nomad, the land hunter, the discontented farmer, the fugitive from justice, and the pursuer of dreams.

There are usually three phases in the process by which a new land is occupied—exploration and discovery, superficial exploitation, and settlement—and these are represented by three groups of agents. First are the explorers. Into the unknown, by sea or land, go those intrepid souls whose main function is the search for information, the discovery of coastlines and waterways, the spying out of the interior of continents. Sometimes they follow a quest of their own; sometimes they go on the mandate of king or country. Columbus and Coronado, Cartier and Lewis and Clark stand for a

host of adventurers. Seldom do these men profit greatly
by their own discoveries, but the tales they tell at the
court of a king or over a tankard of ale in a tavern, and
the accounts which they leave in the pages of reports
and travel books, stir the imagination and the desire
of another group who thereupon follow in their train.
These are not unlike the first, and often they themselves become explorers and discoverers, but their pri-
mary purpose is to exploit, not to explore. They are
the hunters, the trappers, the nomadic traders, the peri-
patetic gold seekers, and with practical and canny purpose they follow in the wake of the earlier breed. There
is romance in their wandering, and they in their turn
fire the spirit of those who come after; but they leave
no permanent deposit of civilization in the land. Their
canoes pass up the streams and down again; they make
use of the trail of the buffalo and the red man; they
appear in an Indian village with trinkets and leave
with furs. In the main they adapt themselves to the
ways of the primitive, knowing full well that with the
passing of the primitive goes also their vocation.

A little less evanescent are such men as those who
built cowpens in the Carolina piedmont, or those who
like Philip Nolan captured wild horses in Texas for the
eastern market, or those who in later years drove cattle
over the great ranges of the West to the cow towns at
the railheads. Basically these also are superficial ex-
ploiters utilizing for a brief time the unoccupied region
and passing with the coming of the real frontier.

The hunters and the traders and the cattle drivers prepare the way for the third group—the actual settlers. These last tread close upon the heels of the second group, driving or following them deeper and deeper into the wilds. They build cabins and permanent forts. They plow the ground and sow seed and thus bind themselves to the soil. They widen trails into roads. Their aims are at variance with those who have gone before and the two groups frequently clash. With the settler comes finally the real zone of the frontier.

So far in this discussion the frontier has received little specific emphasis. The neglect has been deliberate. We have wished to turn attention not so much to the frontier as to the movement that produced it. There is need for a clear distinction between the two phenomena. The westward movement is the whole sweeping process by which the nation and its civilization have been crossing the continent. It created and it perpetuates the spirit that sets apart the East and the West. It has influenced all parts of the country. At a given time the movement may have its head and front in the Mississippi Valley, but back in New England and Virginia are fundamental elements that cannot be divorced from the line of advance. The older regions provide the recruiting ground, the supply stations, the financial support. And in the space between the far east and the far west men struggle to keep the passage clear, to build better roads, to push forward materials to those ahead, and to profit, themselves, by the passage of traffic.

The success of those in front may bring pride or envy, profit or sacrifice, gold dust or deserted farms to those behind the line; may bring to an end a political dynasty or provide commodities for New York City to export. The entire nation is involved in the process, and the towns on the edge of the unconquered are but the pickets of the whole people's advance. The westward movement is a national phenomenon, not merely a local western episode.

The frontier, on the other hand, has a local connotation. It is the edge of the westward movement, the line or zone where rests for the moment the vanguard of progress. It is the margin of settlement, the borderland, dotted with cabins and groups of families—humanity taking root in the soil, with pioneer roads and the beginnings of permanent institutions and physical deposits on the surface of the land.

In the history of America we find the frontier always a region of activity and energy, of struggle and achievement. It is the focus or axis of international conflict and of Indian warfare, and when these rivalries subside and peace lies upon the land it is a zone of no less heroic struggle against natural obstacles—a region where men must grapple barehanded with primitive conditions.

It is striking and picturesque and in a high degree significant, but it is only a part of the story, only a product and element of the greater phenomenon. The westward movement is the tide whereas the frontier is

the line of breakers and white surf. Or, to change the
metaphor, the frontier is the tip of a growing plant, the
farthest point reached by the flowing sap, and the hope
of the plant's continuous growth.

But the story is not all told when we describe the
frontier and the older civilization from which it sprang.
Always it must be remembered that beyond the zone
of the actual frontier was the evanescent but highly
important reconnoitering process—the exploration of
groping and sometimes lost adventurers, the searching
out of Indian trails in an unknown land, the pushing
of canoes around a fresh turn in an untraveled river.
In the land beyond the border men were taking formal
possession, not yet with plow and cabin, but with up-
lifted sword and high-sounding phrases, with perhaps
a cross and the arms of a king left in the solitude of a
visited land, or with leaden plates buried along the
margin of a stream, or initials carved on a tree for later
generations to find.

In the heart of the wilderness shrewd men were visiting the Indian villages in search of trade, and pack-
horse men followed, driving their animals in single file
along the paths of the forest, and now and then came
even the land speculators scouting beyond the border
that they might anticipate their own people and the
law of the realm.

Numerous and bold were these activities, yet nothing
was permanent, and vague and obscure to us are most
of the figures that wandered through the unconquered

West. As Verner W. Crane says of the early Carolina traders:

> Only now and then did they emerge briefly into the light of history, much as when their caravans chanced to pass from the gloom of the vast southern pine forests into some sunny upland savannah.[2]

But dim and shadowy as their forms appear out toward the horizon, the spell they cast was magic and their influence was extraordinary. The call from the wilderness brought the frontiersman out to the border. It was not alone the push from behind but also the lure from the land ahead that kept up the migration into the West and brought about the settlement of the country, and to the men who progressively laid down the farthest frontiers the call could only come from those who had left the road for the Indian trail and taken up the gun and the trap in the land where plowshare and cabin had as yet no place.

One reason for sharply distinguishing between the frontier and the land beyond the border is that there is a vital difference in the character, the purpose, the interests, and the activities of the trader and trapper on the one hand and the settler on the other. The trader was to a greater extent an individualist and a nomad. He was less of a social creature and little interested in the westward movement of a people. Indeed, he dreaded the coming of the settler since it merely meant driving west his fur supply and his Indian associates, and he and the men of influence who backed him and shared his profits were often charged with fomenting frontier attacks to check the westward push. Bacon's Rebellion was in large part an instance of revolt by settlers against the fur trade beyond the border—the revolutionists claiming that the chief men of the colony were selling their blood at the heads of the rivers and refusing them the opportunity to drive back the Indians. The red men for the most part welcomed the trader. He sold them illicit liquor that delighted their primitive gullets, and firearms and ammunition with which they could make war upon unequipped tribes.

The settlers, on the contrary, desired to lay down a permanent civilization and to advance it westward as steadily as possible. The iniquities of the roving trader were visited upon the generations of the established settler. The rum that went into the wilderness secured, by absurd bargains, furs for the traders, but it brought raids of unspeakable savagery to the frontier. The firearms were turned not against the trader who sold them, but against the settler. So the frontiersman hated the Indian and strove constantly to be rid of him by driving him back, meanwhile cursing the trader and protesting to the government against the evils which he perpetrated.

The characteristics of the frontier have been set forth too many times to need repetition here. But there is one element of such appraisal that is clarified by the distinction we have made between the frontier and the land beyond. The lawless bad town of the West has too readily been taken as the type of the frontier. It was lurid and striking, but not necessarily more representative than the Quaker settlement on the border or the peaceful farming community that braved the hardships and the terror of the Indian for the advantages of fresh free soil and a new start. The bad towns were often the points on the border where the wilder life of the exploiter from beyond the frontier impinged upon the border of actual settlement. Such, for example, were traders' towns where whisky was smuggled out to the Indians, and where lawless traffickers and their pack-horse men and assistants made their temporary homes. Such also were the cow towns, where the cattle drives, an element of the unsettled life beyond the frontier, touched the railhead where the real frontier was reaching into the West. And even in the bad towns, though life was held in little esteem and crime was frequent, the community, as the settler became master, tended always to develop a conservative vigilante type which restrained and checked and in the end subjugated the lawless elements.

The pattern laid out upon the land in the early days as the explorer, the exploiter, and the settler in turn moved west is not difficult to visualize. On the eastern margin which first received the Europeans appeared a zone of established civilization, with populous towns, busy trade and comparative wealth, comfort and stability. Farther west, population thinned out and the institutions of civilization diminished. Towns were smaller and farther apart and roads became constantly more primitive until they ended on a line where scattered settlements marked the edge of the zone of occupation. Beyond this frontier was a vague but not unknown country, crossed and recrossed by transient traders, while far off toward the horizon was the terra incognita where the true explorers like Lewis and Clark or the metamorphosed traders like Jedediah Smith were traveling virgin paths.

Such a visualization can of course only be a generalization, but it serves to illustrate the transformation of the land between the oceans. The history of expansion runs no more smoothly than the course of true love, and barren plains and high mountains and such extraordinary stimulants as the discovery of gold caused the westward growth to lag or to accelerate wildly, to veer this way or that or even to turn back upon its course; but these are merely spectacular exceptions due to the fact that neither geography nor humanity nor historic events present homogeneous consistency.

As we picture the Anglo-American westward movement it is well to remember that it was not a solitary phenomenon. There are other frontiers than our own to consider—those that competing nations laid down in the path of our progress. When the English began their colonization in the first half of the seventeenth century they found no rivals in the vicinity. The settlements of Spain in the south and of France in the north lay parallel to the line of our destined expansion.

But about 1670 new conditions arose. In this year the town of Charleston was founded, and with this important event began the movement of Carolinians down into the land which the Spaniard claimed; and in the decade of the 1670's the French turned aside from the Great Lakes and moved southward into the Mississippi Valley, where Marquette and Joliet found traces of English penetration. From then on, the international struggle became acute. The land beyond the border was now also the land between the borders. In the contest of the nations this intervening zone was a no man's land where occurred events whose prime significance is often neglected by the historian. Here Spanish priests and English traders and French agents courted the Indian tribes. There were English in the Indian towns of the Mississippi Valley nearly a hundred years before Boone led settlers into the Kentucky Bluegrass. There were French in the Cherokee villages behind the mountains while the English frontier still lingered in the Piedmont. Indeed, in the international struggle for the continent it was not so much the clashing of frontiers that brought on the fray as it was the sparring of isolated men far beyond the last settlement, sometimes sent by their country but often intriguing for Indian alliance merely in the interests of their own trade. Treaties were made and broken, alliances were formed and dissolved, in a game that was covert and clever and far-reaching in its results. Dr. Henry Woodward, slipping in and out of the "Debatable Land" be-

tween Carolina and the Spanish settlements, Christian
Priber, Jesuit agent of the French in the Cherokee
towns, James Adair, English trader, intriguing to al-
ienate the Choctaw Soulier Rouge from French allegiance, George Croghan and his men among the
northwest Indians, and George Washington, whose
skirmish in the western woods started the last great
French-English struggle in America, are only a few of
the figures in this wilderness game.

Nor did our expansion proceed without casting a
shadow before it. Moving across the land just ahead of
our frontier was the American Indian frontier. It too
was the edge of occupation, but it was not the edge of
expansion. It was a retreating frontier and represented
an inverted movement—a tragedy in the life of a race.
In essence the two borderlines were antitheses. Whatever there was of growth or glamour or victory in the
advance of the one was matched by loss and humilia-
tion and defeat in the withdrawal of the other.

In the course of years the process of western expansion assumes a new aspect. As the elements shift westward to the Pacific the colorful contrasts gradually dim.
Each phase of the movement eclipses the one before
and quieter tones pervade the scene. Terra incognita
becomes crisscrossed with trappers' paths; the settler
follows and crowds the trapper toward the horizon.
Rival nations roll back on each side like the waters of
the Red Sea. Indian warriors succumb to their fate.
The frontier climbs the mountains and drops down to

the western sea. The neglected and less desirable portions of the land are filled in. The frontier is gone. But population is still fluid and men continue to go west. The comforts and refinements of life move toward the far coast. East is still East; the West remains a legend and a challenge; and the transmutation of traits and ideas goes on across the continent. Thus the long and yet unified story presents itself.

Little attempt has been made in this paper to do more than evaluate and associate the physical elements and note their progress across the country. With respect to the importance of our national expansion in its relation, both direct and reactive, to political, economic, and social life, and in its effect upon American characteristics, no one has gone beyond the vision of Professor Turner a generation ago. His finely interpretative mind envisaged the whole movement in time and space and quality. If later writers have fallen into more restrictive interpretations or followed down tempting bypaths without reference to the general map, the fault is not his but ours. We need to orient ourselves once more on the broad lines of his basic interpretation. And if we are to make any progress beyond, we must arrive at a reappraisal of the nature of the factors and forces of the entire process. We must see in its full unity the expansion of a people. We must study in their proper relations the explorer, the nomadic hunter and trader, and the pioneer settler, and see them each giving way in turn to more conservative and stable forces.

We must consider the interplay of rival borderlands, retreating Indian lines, and advancing Americans; all these with their peculiar manifestations must be related to the ever-increasing domain of stabilized civilization destined in the end to cover the entire land.

Instead of a kaleidoscopic series of pictures we then can create a moving portrayal of the metamorphosis of a land and its people, a symphonic story in which are harmonized the parts played by many kinds of men and women in a sweeping movement that gives expression and meaning to the whole of American life. Groping and uncertain beginnings prepare the way for a long period marked by the discord of sharply contrasted elements until finally the theme changes into a more smooth intermingling of ideas and manners in which the West has been gradually but steadily tamed, quieted, and civilized by being overtaken by eastern influences, while the East has been constantly jarred out of its ruts, energized, and forced to keep alive by the persistence of the western mood. Divergent forces will probably always keep us sectional and heterogeneous, but if there ever is discernible an amalgamated American spirit it will be explained only after a clear and comprehensive appreciation of the interrelated phases and elements of the westward movement and a study of their resultant influence on the individual and the nation.

NOTES

[1] John C. Parish, "The Persistence of the Westward Movement," *Yale Review*, XV (April, 1926) , 461–477.

[2] Verner W. Crane, *The Southern Frontier*, pp. 39–40.

THE EMERGENCE OF THE
IDEA OF MANIFEST
DESTINY

——◦《 》◦——

ONE OF THE influential forces operating in America's advance westward to the Pacific was the idea which we speak of as Manifest Destiny. In a large sense this may be interpreted as referring to the confident and persistent belief in the future supremacy of America in a variety of fields—political, industrial, financial, and cultural. In a more specific form it refers to a belief in an inevitable territorial expansion, particularly toward the Pacific Ocean, or, as it was called in early days, the South Sea. It is to the specific phase that we shall devote our attention.

This imperial vision was not so much a cause as it was a product of our early westward expansion. Nevertheless, once it had taken form in the minds of Americans, it stimulated in extraordinary fashion their movement across the continent. The idea did not receive its distinguishing name—Manifest Destiny—until toward the middle of the nineteenth century. In fact, the term appears only three years before the national advance had made us possessors of our entire Pacific

coastline exclusive of Alaska. But its roots reach far
back into the beginnings of American history and the
idea was in clear and potent existence more than half
a century before it became a slogan in the press and
in the halls of Congress.

It is almost universally associated with its final expression just before and during the Mexican War.
Julius W. Pratt, after a careful investigation of the first
appearance of the term, reports that the earliest use
of the phrase was in an article in the *Democratic Review* for July–August, 1845, wherein the editor speaks
of "the fulfilment of our manifest destiny to overspread
the continent allotted by Providence for the free development of our yearly multiplying millions." The
same editor, John L. O'Sullivan, writing for the New
York *Morning News* in December, 1845, urged our
claim to Oregon in these words: "And that claim is by
the right of our manifest destiny to overspread and to
possess the whole of the continent which Providence
has given us for the development of the great experiment of liberty and federated self-government." The
phrase apparently caught the attention of a Congressman who carried it to the floor of the House of Representatives, whence it began echoing back and forth
across the country.[1] The slogan played its part in the
stirring scenes of the three years from 1845 to 1848 during which period we admitted Texas into the Union,
received title to Oregon, waged a war that ended with

[1] For notes see pages 75–77.

the acquisition of two-fifths of the territory of Mexico, and came into possession of our western oceanic front-age. Thus equipped with a name to conjure with, the idea has continued to hold a place in our national consciousness.

The idea, however, was much older than the name. In his significant book on the War of 1812, Mr. Pratt, whom I have cited above, discusses the flare of western nationalism and desire for expansion that brought on our second war with England and maintains that, not with the controversies of the 'thirties and 'forties came the dawn of the idea of Manifest Destiny, but with the War of 1812, and he mentions even earlier enthusiasts, like Jefferson.[2]

It is the object of this paper to carry the investigation back still farther and to show that the actual emergence of the idea was in the eighteenth century, that it found a seedbed in the advance of the colonial frontier, that it accompanied as a potential force the struggle for independence, that it came into recognition and clear expression by numerous observers both at home and abroad during our first experiences as a separate nation, and that it received partial fulfillment and marked stimulus in the Louisiana Purchase of 1803.

During the decades and generations when the frontier was pushing westward from the coasts of New England into the valley of the Connecticut River and the plains of central New York, and from the tidewater lands of Virginia and Carolina into the Piedmont and the mountain valleys of the Alleghenies, a spirit was being created and a force generated that was to mean much to the American people. Yet for nearly a century and a half there was little indication of anything but local and immediate objectives. The activities of the western colonists were largely uncorrelated. The variety of motives and purposes, the differences of political and economic controls and policies, and the wide spaces between frontier outposts served to make their advance a movement of unassociated elements. Furthermore, they faced, in the path of their ultimate expansion, a determined and energetic enemy in the persons of the French.

Nevertheless, their routes were in general parallel, their experiences similar, and only a readjustment of conditions was necessary to give them unity and a clear field ahead, and to provide a basis out of which such an idea as Manifest Destiny could emerge. The readjustment came with the French and Indian War.

This last Anglo-French struggle in America cleared the pathway of the English west to the Mississippi. The French, eliminated from the continent, were replaced beyond the Mississippi by Spain—a weaker nation that did not for years even occupy the trans-Mississippi heritage. The war, furthermore, helped to coalesce the experiences and interests of the American colonists. Most important of all, it brought a train of events that led to conflict between England and her colonies and the final independence of thirteen of the colonial establishments.

With the defeat of the French came an immediate pressure of people into the more easily accessible portions of the land beyond the Alleghenies. Already, in the 1750's, a trans-Allegheny settlement had sprung up in the Monongahela Valley.³ Before the close of the war, the British commander at Fort Pitt, Colonel Bouquet, caused great resentment by prohibiting the advance of settlers into the region of the forks of the Ohio.⁴ He based his action on the need of preserving treaty obligations with the Indians and was sincerely fearful that the push of settlers would upset the tribes and bring untold horrors. This fear of an Indian war was realized in 1763, a few months after the signature of the treaty of peace. Pontiac's war, widespread in extent, confirmed the decision of the British government to set up a western limit to the expansion of the settlers, and in October the Proclamation of 1763 forbade the granting of lands beyond the sources of streams flowing into the Atlantic. In the flush of enthusiasm of colonial governments and back settlers, this restraining order came as a cruel blow. From then on a struggle took place between determined expansionists on the one hand and a harassed British government on the other. An Indian boundary arranged with the tribes by the Superintendents of Indian Affairs (Sir William Johnson and Captain John Stuart) was set up, revised, and pushed westward in the course of the struggle. As fast as a line was defined, settlers broke over it, Indians protested, new treaties and new lines were established.

In 1765, Cherokee chiefs complained to Governor Bull of South Carolina against misinterpretations of the boundary: "Now the whites say it is Broadies plantation. Next they will say Twelve Mile River."[5] In 1769, warriors of the same nation sent word to Superintendent Stuart: "The White People pay no regard to all our talks that we have had. They are in Bodies in the middle of our Hunting Grounds some of our people were as far as the Long Island on Holsons River but they were obliged to come home for the whole Nation is full of Hunters, and the Guns rattling every way and Horse Paths on the River both up and down we are sure they have settled the Land a great Way on this Side of the Line."[6] Stuart toiled manfully with his task of restraining the settlers, but with scant success. Lord Dartmouth, in charge of colonial affairs in 1773, wrote to him that he hoped for Stuart's success with the Cherokees. "At the same time [he continued] I am free to confess that I very much doubt whether that dangerous spirit of unlicensed emigration into the Interior parts of America can be effectually restrained by any authority whatever."[7] And Lord Dunmore, Governor of Virginia, wrote to Dartmouth in 1775: "But my Lord I have learnt from experience that the established Authority of any government in America, and the policy of Government at home, are both insufficient to restrain the Americans and they do and will remove as their avidity and restlessness incite them."[8]

The facts given so far merely show the persistent ad-

vance of inconspicuous persons—a movement of people who clearly had no realization of a great mission
to be performed or a vast continent to be won. They
moved by small advances, motivated largely by their
own personal desires. But the accumulation of these
little activities of men who saw no large significance to
their advance became a tide of migration without
which national ambition and territorial increase would
have been but a dream and a mockery. Let us in-
quire, however, if there were not here and there men
of larger means and more roving intellects who saw
beyond the immediate goal, realized the implications
of the process, and took fire from the possibilities their
imaginations conjured before them. Go back in the pre-
Revolutionary period to the year 1755. Practically a
century and a half had passed since the first founding
by Englishmen in America. All the thirteen colonies
had come into existence and still the frontier lingered
east of the Allegheny Mountains. Listen to the pro-
nouncement of Robert Dinwiddie, peppery Governor
of Virginia, in a report to the Board of Trade: "Virg'a
resumes its ancient Breadth, and has not other Limits
to the West y'n w't its first Royal Charter assigned to
it, and y't is to the So. Sea, including the Isl'd of California."[9]

And Thomas Pownall, later Governor of Massachusetts, wrote home to England on behalf of a new colony
he was projecting south of Lake Erie. Among the manuscripts of the Huntington Library are his map and de-

scription of his enterprise. One statement rings out with startling clearness: "This [colony] woud also be in time ye *Center of ye Manufacturers of this Continent* which if the English do not possess and make so, the French will. Lett that strike you for 'tis beyond all doubt."[10] Today the factories of western Pennsylvania and Ohio attest the validity of his prophecy.

And young John Adams, twenty years old and just out of Harvard, with more than seventy years of life ahead of him, wrote, in 1755, his views on the transfer of empire.

[England, he said,] is now the greatest nation upon the globe. Soon after the Reformation, a few people came over into this new world for conscience sake. Perhaps this apparently trivial incident may transfer the great seat of empire into America. It looks likely to me: for if we can remove the turbulent Gallicks, our people, according to the exactest computations, will in another century become more numerous than England itself. Should this be the case, since we have, I may say, all the naval stores of the nation in our hands, it will be easy to obtain the mastery of the seas; and then the united force of all Europe will not be able to subdue us. The only way to keep us from setting up for ourselves is to disunite us.[11]

In this same year 1755, there appeared in print, though written four years before, the following comments of Benjamin Franklin.

Thus there are suppos'd to be now upwards of One Million *English* souls in *North-America.* . . . This Million doubling, suppose but once in 25 Years, will, in another Century, be more than the People of *England* and the greatest Number of *Englishmen* will be on this Side the Water. What an Accession of Power to the *British* Empire by Sea as well as Land! What Increase of Trade and Navigation! What Numbers of Ships and Seamen! . . . How important an Affair then to *Britain* is the present Treaty for settling the Bounds between her colonies and the *French,* and how careful should she be to secure Room enough, since on the Room depends so much the Increase of her People.[12]

This was twenty years before the first shot was fired in the American Revolution. Perhaps Manifest Destiny in these two intervening decades may best be studied by examining Franklin's sayings and doings. It will be noted that, while both Adams and Franklin foresaw the tremendous increase of population and growth of power in America, they differed greatly in point of view. Adams more than hints at separation and an American Empire. Franklin, however, sees the increase in numbers and power resulting entirely in the upbuilding of a greater British nation. His imperial vision is altogether an English one. This continued to be characteristic of him until he was disillusioned by his experiences in England just before the Revolution. In January, 1760, apropos of the fall of Quebec, he wrote to his friend Lord Kames:

No one can more sincerely rejoice than I do, on the reduction of Canada; and this is not merely as I am a colonist, but as I am a Briton. I have long been of the opinion, that the *foundations of the future grandeur and stability of the British empire lie in America.* . . . I am therefore by no means for restoring Canada. If we keep it, all the country from the St. Lawrence to the Mississippi will in another century be filled with British people. Britain herself will become vastly more populous, by the immense increase of its commerce; the Atlantic sea will be covered with your trading ships; and your naval power, thence continually increasing will extend your influence round the whole globe, and awe the world.[13]

Thus spoke an Englishman of the destinies of his nation in America. In the same year arose the question whether England should retain Canada or give it back to France. William Burke advocated the relinquishment, maintaining that if "the people of our colonies find no check from Canada they will extend themselves without bounds into the inland parts. They will increase infinitely from all causes. What the consequences will be to have a numerous, hardy, independent people, possessed of a strong country, communicating little or not at all with England," he left to conjecture.[14] Franklin answered him in an extended pamphlet in which he agreed as to the probable increase of inhabitants.[15] But he did not anticipate separation. Both men were subjects of Great Britain—both saw clearly the possibilities in the West; but Burke feared the tendency toward revolt and the transfer of imperial possibilities to an independent America, while Franklin, a native of America, stoutly denied the danger.

The affair of the Stamp Act, however, somewhat shook his confidence and his self-restraint, and in April he burst out rather frankly in a letter to Lord Kames.

He loved England, he said, and wished for the continuance of Union on which alone England's prosperity could be secured.

As to America [he added], the advantages of such a union to her are not so apparent. She may suffer at present under the arbitrary power of this country [he was in England at the time]; she may suffer for a while in a separation from it; but these are temporary evils that she will outgrow. Scotland and Ireland are differently circumstanced. Confined by the sea, they can scarcely increase in numbers, wealth and strength, so as to overbalance England. But America, an immense territory, favoured by Nature with all advantages of climate, soil, great navigable rivers, and lakes, &/c. must become a great country, populous and mighty; and will in a less time than is generally conceived, be able to shake off any shackles that may be imposed on her, and perhaps place them on the imposers.[16]

These were bold words—too bold to suit Franklin's ambitions. He had been interested for a dozen years and more in projects of new colonies in the western part of America, and if concessions were to be granted for such enterprises he must not antagonize the British administration. In August of the same year, 1767, he wrote from London to his son, describing a talk he had had with Lord Shelburne and Lord Conway, then in the ascendancy in the ministry. He took the opportunity of urging upon them the plan of himself and associates for a settlement in the Illinois country. He expatiated on its various advantages, and named among others "raising a strength there which on occasion of a future war, might easily be poured down the Mississippi upon the lower country, and into the Bay of Mexico, to be used against Cuba or Mexico itself."[17]

In 1769 he again emphasized British interests in America. Describing the widespread habit of reading in America he said: "It must, I think, be a pleasing reflection to those who write either for the benefit of the present age or of posterity, to find their audience increasing with the increase of our colonies, and their language extending itself beyond the narrow bounds of these islands, to a continent larger than all Europe, and to future empire as fully peopled, which Britain may one day probably possess in those vast western regions."[18]

But Franklin's hopes proved futile either for British empire in western America or for his own colonial ventures in the same region. After long years in England he came home in 1775 completely disillusioned and proceeded to translate his dreams of empire in America into new and quite different forms.

About four years before, a young man graduating from Princeton—Philip Freneau by name—wrote his fervid ideas into a poem, "The Rising Glory of America." In the dialogue form of this poem Eugenio says:

> But come, Leander, since we know the past
> And present glory of this empire wide,
> What hinders to pervade with searching eye
> The mystic scenes of dark futurity?

Say, shall we ask what empires yet must rise,
What kingdoms, pow'rs and states where now are seen
But dreary wastes and awful solitude,
Where melancholy sits with eye forlorn
And hopes the day when Britain's sons shall spread
Dominion to the north and south and west
Far from th' Atlantic to Pacific shores?

And Acasto replies:
                         I see, I see
A thousand kingdoms rais'd, cities and men
Num'rous as sand upon the ocean shore;
Th' Ohio then shall glide by many a town
Of note: and where the Mississippi stream
By forests shaded now runs weeping on,
Nations shall grow and states not less in fame
Than Greece and Rome of old. . . .[19]

With this epilogue to the first act, let us drop the
curtain while the American colonies busy themselves
with shifting scenery during the American Revolution.
In the second act the cast of characters will not be
wholly new, but the actors will play new roles. Franklin and Adams, arranging the terms of peace, will discuss a new kind of empire. Shelburne will come briefly
and sadly upon the stage. A little later, Freneau will
reappear, waging valiant and vitriolic battle as editor
of the *National Gazette* for the political party of the
greatest early apostle of Manifest Destiny—Thomas
Jefferson.

During the engrossing years of the Revolution, the
minds of Americans were fixed on the conflict. The
West scarcely drew their attention. A lone figure in the

person of George Rogers Clark—talking over his plans with Governor Patrick Henry of Virginia and then moving with a few followers out into the wilderness of the Illinois country—presents a notable exception to this neglect.

When Cornwallis surrendered, however, and it became evident that the thirteen commonwealths were making good their announcement in the Declaration of Independence, men's spirits and minds stirred to a new conception. Prior to the war there were some who, like the young Adams, clearly thought in terms of the possible future development of an independent America. Even Franklin, in one instance, had allowed himself to hint such a possibility. But usually this abortive patriotism was inarticulate because of a wise caution, or because of a readiness to further British imperial hopes as long as Britain gave adequate justice and freedom to her American sons.

But the proud and patriotic spirit of Britishers in England and America, who looked forward with faith and imagination to the growth of numbers and of power on the new continent, to an inevitable expansion westward, and to the acquisition and administration of a great continental empire, clearly represents the idea of Manifest Destiny even though a new and local nation, instead of the old, was destined to enjoy the benefits. To make it an idea of and for America alone, there was needed only the independence of the United States and their assumption of a natural heritage. Now independence had been secured, and we turn to a phase in which those Americans who had concealed their hopes, or who had talked of the development of the West in terms of British imperial greatness as a cover for local independent ambitions, could speak without restraint. And those of the colonists who had with sincere love of country seen visions of British glory in America, now could and must replace that vision with a not less glorious dream for the new nation.

Men of all nations saw the possibilities ahead of the victors. Lord Shelburne, who from long association knew, as perhaps no other English statesman, the value of the region his country was losing, stated in Parliament that when the colonial independence "should be established, the sun of England might be said to have set," but added that "it was his resolution to improve the twilight, and to prepare for the rising of England's sun again."[20]

Some of the newspapers of the British Isles took the blow with less philosophy. The *Morning Post* of London, in December, 1782, having learned of the preliminary peace provisions, remarked:

As soon as the Thirteen Colonies are established in the form of a separate state, tens of thousands will emigrate from all parts of Europe and repair the losses of the war with a rapid increase of population. The pride of empire will awaken, and conquests will be multiplied on neighboring borders. Hallifax [*sic*] and Nova Scotia must soon fall; Canada must follow; the fisheries of Newfoundland

will, in time be engrossed by themselves, and then they will
direct their strength against the islands. Florida and all the
Spanish possessions on the banks of the Mississippi will
fall before them; and as they increase in power, that power
will reach the limits of the Southern Ocean, and dispossess
the Europeans of every hold upon the great continent of
America. Such will be the wise, the blessed effects of sepa-
rating them from Great Britain; and such the consequences,
that in less than a quarter of a century may overturn all
the political systems of the old world.[21]

In France astute leaders saw the trend of events.
Luzerne wrote to Vergennes: "The Americans in pushing their possessions as far as the Lake of the Woods,
are preparing for their remote posterity a communication with the Pacific."[22] Vergennes—wily old diplomat—
looked on with interested eyes. He probably recalled
how he had warned Great Britain when that country—twenty years before—had taken Canada away from
France. "Delivered," he had said, "from a neighbor
whom they always feared, your other colonies will soon
discover, that they stand no longer in need of your
protection. You will call on them to contribute toward
supporting the burthen which they have helped to
bring on you, they will answer you by shaking off all
dependence."[23]

He had seen his prophecy exactly fulfilled. But now
although his country had helped materially in bringing independence to the colonies, he was not so happy
to see them advance into the West and he talked with
Count Aranda, Minister of Spain, of ways to check and

limit the westward ambitions of the new nation in the making of the treaty of peace.

It must be remembered that, at the close of the French and Indian War, France had ceded the trans-Mississippi regions and New Orleans to her friend and ally, Spain. The Revolution brought no change in the land beyond the river. Spanish operations against England in the West, however, during the late years of the war, left Spain in possession not only of the far bank of the river but also of various points on the east side of the stream and the gulf posts of Mobile and Pensacola.

Spain had made no alliance with the thirteen American states and was in truth jealous and fearful of their advance. She hoped to keep her conquests east of the Mississippi and was even alarmed for the safety of her internal provinces. Count Aranda gave pointed expression to this alarm in a memoir to the King of Spain. There has been some controversy over the authenticity of the memoir,[24] and at least two versions have been published. One is as follows:

This Republic has been born, as it were a pygmy; she needed the help and assistance of no less than two such powerful states as France and Spain, in order to conquer her independence; but a day will come when she will be a giant, a veritable awe-inspiring colossus in those regions; she will forget the favors that she has received; she will only think of her own interest and her own convenience. . . . The first step of the new nation will be to seize Florida, so as to dominate the Gulf of Mexico. She will then conquer New Spain and the vast empire, the defence of which will be rendered impossible to us, as we shall not be able to struggle against a powerful nation, established on the same continent. . . ."[25]

Another shrewd Spaniard, Martín Navarro, intendant in Louisiana for many years, made a similar comment when, in 1788, he likened the American nation to a newborn giant who would not rest satisfied until he had extended his domains across the continent and bathed his vigorous young limbs in the placid waters of the Pacific.[26]

Six years later Baron Carondelet, Spanish governor of Louisiana, was sending home frantic letters describing the aggressive spirit of the Americans and the menace to Spanish possessions west of the Mississippi. He characterized them as a people "hostile to all subjection, advancing and multiplying in the silence of peace and almost unknown, with a prodigious rapidity, ever since the independence of the United States was recognized. . . ."[27] And in time [he said] they will demand the possession of the rich mines of the interior provinces of the very kingdom of Mexico."[28]

If England and France and Spain read the portents so clearly, it is not surprising that the vision flourished in the minds of Americans in the years that followed the Revolution. Unhindered now by proclamations, settlers poured through the Allegheny passes and down the Ohio in unprecedented numbers to fill up the land of Kentucky and Tennessee and the old northwest. In books devoted to geographic description the idea of Manifest Destiny found expression with great frequency. Among the most important books of this type in the late eighteenth century was the *American Geography* written by Jedidiah Morse, a New Englander. Published in 1789, it ran through many editions and without doubt received a very wide reading. Morse included an account of the "Western Country," as he calls the trans-Allegheny. He described this region as it existed in the 1780's and incidentally made comments on the land that lay beyond the river in the possession of Spain. He anticipated a process by which Americans would cross the Mississippi, carrying their American habits with them into a foreign domain. They would still be Americans in fact, he maintained, although nominally the subjects of Spain. What a clear prediction of the process that went on so definitely in the next century when men from the United States filtering into Texas, New Mexico, and California, became Spanish or Mexican citizens but proved to be Americans under the skin in the wars of 1836 and 1846! Morse then proceeded to give his views as to the destiny of America. "Besides," he said:

it is well known that empire has been traveling from east to west. Probably her last and broadest seat will be America. Here the sciences and the arts of civilized life are to receive their highest improvement. Here civil and religious liberty are to flourish, unchecked by the cruel hand of civil or ecclesiastical tyranny. Here Genius, aided by all the improvements of former ages, is to be exerted in humanizing mankind—in expanding and enriching their minds with religious and philosophical knowledge, and in planning and executing a form of government, which shall involve all the excellencies of former governments, with as few of their defects as is consistent with the imperfection of human affairs, and which shall be calculated to protect and unite, in a manner consistent with the natural rights of mankind, the largest empire that ever existed. Elevated with these prospects, which are not merely the visions of fancy, we cannot but anticipate the period, as not far distant, when the AMERICAN EMPIRE will comprehend millions of souls, west of the Mississippi. Judging upon probable grounds, the Mississippi was never designed as the western boundary of the American empire. The God of nature never intended that some of the best part of his earth should be inhabited by the subjects of a monarch 4000 miles from them. And may we not venture to predict, that, when the rights of mankind shall be more fully known, and the knowledge of them is fast increasing both in Europe and America, the power of European potentates will be confined to Europe, and their present American dominions become like the United States, free, sovereign, and independent empires.[29]

Thus, early in the year 1789, before Washington was inaugurated as President of the United States, the prophet Jedidiah sums up in one paragraph an explicit statement of the idea of Manifest Destiny, and a prediction of the rise of the Latin American states to independence and freedom.

Three years later, Gilbert Imlay, a Kentuckian, published a *Topographical Description of the Western Territory of North America*. He predicted that "posterity will not deem it extraordinary, should they find the country settled quite across to the Pacific Ocean, in less than another century."[30]

He really knew little about the Far West. Nobody did in 1792 for the simple reason that no white man had yet traversed America in the central portion of the continent. Hence we need not be surprised at the naïveté of his remark that crossing to the western sea should not be difficult, "as it does not appear that the ridges of hills which divide the waters of the Pacific Ocean from the waters of the Mississippi, are either so high or so rugged as the Allegheny Mountains."[31]

He seems calmly to ignore the presence and authority of the Spaniards beyond the Mississippi or the English in Canada, and pictures the Americans as spreading by way of the rivers to the sea in all directions, to the Atlantic, Hudson's Bay, the Arctic, and the Pacific. "Thus in the center of the earth, governing by the laws of reason and humanity, we seem calculated to become at once the emporium and protectors of the world."[32]

In a later edition in the same decade he adds the suggestion that it is "puerile in the United States to think of making the seat of their government permanent upon the Potowmac . . . when it is obvious that posterity will, in the course of a century at farthest, remove it to the Mississippi." He suggests either Lake Pepin or St. Anthony Falls as a proper place for the capital.[33]

Despite the dreams of book writers, however, Spain still held the west bank of the Mississippi, and it took

a dozen years after the treaty of peace for the United
States to persuade her to give up even her claims to
land on the eastern side.

But how did the idea of Manifest Destiny appear to
men associated more directly with the government of
the new nation? Washington's faith in the West is amply
attested not only by his words, but also by his extensive purchase of western lands, and his efforts to bind
the East and West together by improvement in water
transportation. Patrick Henry and many another east-
erner speculated in lands on the Mississippi, and Henry
Knox and Rufus King and even Alexander Hamilton,
though apparently little stirred by the frontier, found
themselves greatly intrigued by the proposal of the adventurer Miranda that the United States participate in
the freeing and reorganizing of Latin American states.

But of all public men in the period following the
Revolution, Thomas Jefferson serves most admirably
for our study. Jefferson had always been tremendously
interested in the West. in his *Notes on Virginia,* written
in 1781, before the colonies had actually acquired their
independence, he gave evidence of a most careful study
of the Missouri and Rio Grande river systems and of
the roads and distances in the Spanish land beyond the
Mississippi.[34] In 1783 he wrote the often-quoted letter
to George Rogers Clark: "I find they have subscribed
a very large sum of money in England for exploring the
country from the Mississippi to California. they pre-
tend it is only to promote knowledge. I am afraid they

have thoughts of colonizing into that quarter. some of us have been talking here in a feeble way of making the attempt to search that country. but I doubt whether we have enough of that kind of spirit to raise the money. how would you like to lead such a party? tho I am afraid our prospect is not worth asking the question."[35] Thenceforth for twenty years he clung to his project of a transcontinental expedition and with the success of the Lewis and Clark Expedition he found his ambition fulfilled.

One of the significant points in Jefferson's letter to Clark is his fear of England's getting control in the land beyond the Mississippi. The two most serious threats to American destiny in the West were (1) occupation of the land by either England or France, and (2) separation from the United States of the rapidly developing territories between the Alleghenies and the Mississippi.

As early as 1784 Jefferson expressed his alarm at the tendency toward separatism in Kentucky, and he never ceased to protest against its cause in the neglect of western interests by the federal government.[36] In this same year, after seeing his proposal of a plan of government for the trans-Allegheny region enacted, with some modifications, into a law known generally as Jefferson's Ordinance, he left for France, where he succeeded Benjamin Franklin as diplomatic representative of the United States. He did not return from Europe until 1789, but his absence from the United States did not divert his mind from thoughts of the West.

In a letter to a friend in 1786 he wrote what seems to me to be the key to his policy with regard to the expansion of America:

Our present federal limits are not too large for good government. . . Our confederacy must be viewed as the nest, from which all America, North and South, is to be peopled. We should take care too, not to think it for the interest of that great continent to press too soon on the Spaniards. Those countries cannot be in better hands. My fear is that they are too feeble to hold them till our population can be sufficiently advanced to gain it from them piece by piece. The navigation of the Mississippi we must have. This is all we are as yet ready to receive.[37]

Here is a conception as vast as the hemisphere, adapted to the needs and possibilities of the political situation, and contemplated with the unhurried faith of a philosopher. Spain must be forced to grant the use of the Mississippi River or else the trans-Allegheny would separate from the Union and take matters into its own hands. But, the right of navigation being secured, it was the part of wisdom to bar out England and France by leaving Spain, a feebler nation, in possession of the land beyond the river until America herself should be able to take it from her piece by piece.

In the same year, commenting on an article on America prepared for the French *Encyclopédie Politique,* Jefferson pointed out that the area of the United States was about a million square miles, and that the more populated portions contained about ten persons to the square mile. Experience had shown him, he said, that

when areas reached this figure, "the inhabitants become uneasy, as too much compressed, and go off in
great numbers to search for vacant country. Within 40
years the whole territory will be peopled at that rate.
We may fix that then as the term beyond which the
people of those states will not be restrained within their
present limits. . . . The soil of the country on the western side of the Mississippi, it's climate, & it's vicinity
to the U.S. point it out as the first that will receive
population from that nest. The present occupiers will
have just force enough to repress & and restrain the
emigrations to a certain degree of consistence."[38]

When we contemplate these words of Jefferson it is
hard to believe that his persistent efforts to further the
exploration of the Pacific West were based on mere
academic and scientific curiosity. While he was in Paris
he talked with John Ledyard, a far-wandering Connecticut Yankee, encouraged him in an unsuccessful
plan to penetrate western America by way of Russia
and Siberia, and later secured Ledyard's promise to
push westward from Kentucky, when he should return
from a trip he was embarking upon into the region of
the upper Nile. But Ledyard never came out of the
Nile country.[39]

When in the winter of 1789–90 Jefferson returned
to America and became Secretary of State, he needed
to be more discreet; also he was faced with practical
questions that could not wait the slow process of time.
The Nootka Sound controversy brought England and

Spain to the verge of war, and Jefferson was greatly
alarmed at the possibility of Great Britain's becoming
possessed of Louisiana and Florida. He also felt that
the situation, being desperate for Spain, might bring
concessions to the United States, so he wrote our diplomatic representatives in Madrid suggesting that Spain
might well gain our friendship now by granting us the
navigation of the Mississippi,[40] and he went so far as to
raise the question of a grant of the Floridas and New
Orleans to the United States in exchange for a guaranty
to Spain of the trans-Mississippi region.[41] But the war
scare blew over and the idea of the acquisition of the
Floridas was postponed a decade, when it became the
opening offer in a negotiation that brought us the much
larger cession of the whole of Louisiana.

Passing over the decade of the 1790's, let us study the
relation of Jefferson's ideas of Manifest Destiny to the
events of his presidency. In 1801, writing very confidentially to Monroe, he said with respect to the expansion of America: "However our present interests may
restrain us within our limits, it is impossible not to look
forward to distant times, when our rapid multiplica-
tion will expand it beyond those limits, & cover the
whole northern if not the southern continent."[42]

But "distant times" was a phrase that was ill suited
to the process of American expansion. Stirring events
were around the corner. Already Jefferson had heard
that France had acquired Louisiana from Spain and
probably East and West Florida as well, and he had

sent Livingston to Paris with instructions to buy from the new and unwelcome owner New Orleans and the Floridas. On October 28, 1802, Livingston reported that a suggestion had been made to him by Joseph Bonaparte for the sale of the whole of Louisiana.[43] It apparently made no great impression on Livingston. Perhaps it meant more to Jefferson than historians have granted. At all events, Jefferson, who had learned as well of the closing of the mouth of the Mississippi by Spanish officials, took two almost simultaneous actions. On January 11, 1803, he recommended to Congress that Monroe be sent to Paris to reinforce Livingston, and on January 18 he recommended to the same body that an expedition be sent to explore the region west to the Pacific Ocean. In the latter message we find these words: "The appropriation of $2500 'for the purpose of extending the external commerce of the United States' while understood and considered by the Executive as giving the legislative sanction, would cover the undertaking from notice and prevent the obstructions which interested individuals might otherwise previously prepare in its way."[44]

Within four months Livingston and Monroe had signed a treaty for the cession of Louisiana and New Orleans. Jefferson's hesitation, now that the land had been acquired, arose only from his question of the need of putting through a constitutional amendment before final ratification of the purchase. But events were moving faster than he was wont to move. He gave way gracefully and one great step had been taken in the process which he had so often advocated but which he had expected would cover a long period of years.

What about the Floridas? Jefferson was soon persuaded by Livingston and Monroe that they were really included in the Louisiana Purchase, but in case they were not he did not worry since, as he wrote to Breckenridge, "These claims will be a subject of negociation with Spain, and if, as soon as she is at war, we push them strongly with one hand, holding out a price in the other, we shall certainly obtain the Floridas, and all in good time."[45]

With the future fulfillment of this prediction I shall not deal. I close the case with 1803, and recall Jefferson's theory that piece by piece the Spanish dominions would fall into our possession. The interference of France had precipitated events that resulted in the acquisition of the first and largest piece. In good time the rest would follow. I am only interested now in showing how clearly the idea of Manifest Destiny had emerged. Adams' youthful prophecy was coming to pass. Franklin's vision was materializing but with a different control. Foreign commentators and observant travelers could laud their own prophetic wisdom, and Jefferson's two great specters, namely, separatism and European interference in the West, had lost their terror, for neither of them held much menace after the great event of 1803.

For more than forty years Manifest Destiny was still

to remain unchristened, but the emergence of the idea was now an accomplished fact, and its appeal for good or for ill had become firmly planted and a powerful force in American life.

NOTES

[1] Mr. Pratt's article from which these facts and quotations are taken appeared in the *American Historical Review*, XXXII (July, 1927), 795–798, under the title "The Origin of 'Manifest Destiny'."

[2] Julius W. Pratt, *Expansionists of 1812* (New York, 1925), p. 14.

[3] Alfred P. James, "The First English-Speaking Trans-Appalachian Frontier," *Mississippi Valley Historical Review*, XVII (June, 1930), 55–71.

[4] Clarence W. Alvord, *The Mississippi Valley in British Politics* (Cleveland, 1917), I, 121–122.

[5] Talk from Cherokee chiefs to William Bull, July 11, 1765. British Public Record Office, C.O., 5:66, pp. 829–832.

[6] British Public Record Office, C.O., 5:70, p. 595.

[7] Dartmouth to Stuart, March 3, 1773. British Public Record Office, C.O., 5:74, pp. 63–66.

[8] Reuben G. Thwaites and Louise P. Kellogg, *Documentary History of Dunmore's War* (Madison, Wis., 1905), p. 371.

[9] R. A. Brock (ed.), *Official Record of Robert Dinwiddie*, I, 380.

[10] Manuscript Division, Huntington Library, Loudoun Papers 716.

[11] Charles Francis Adams (ed.), *The Works of John Adams* (Boston, 1856), I, 23.

[12] Albert H. Smyth (ed.), *The Writings of Benjamin Franklin* (New York, 1907), III, 71–72.

[13] *Ibid.*, IV, 4.

[14] George E. Howard, *Preliminaries of the Revolution* (New York, 1905, p. 8.

[15] *The Interests of Great Britain Considered with Regard to Her Colonies.* See Smyth, *Writings of Franklin*, IV, 33–82.

[16] Smyth, *Writings of Benjamin Franklin*, V, 21.

[17] *Ibid.*, p. 46.

[18] *Ibid.*, V, 209.

[19] Fred L. Pattee, *The Poems of Philip Freneau* (Princeton, N. J., 1902), I, 73–74. The poem was the joint product of Freneau and H. H. Brackenbridge. As to the probable contribution of Freneau see *ibid.*, I, xxi.

[20] Thomas C. Hansard, *Parliamentary History of England*, XXIII, cols. 193, 194.

[21] Quoted in Eunice Wead, "British Public Opinion of the Peace with America, 1782," *American Historical Review*, XXXIV (April, 1929), 522.

[22] Justin Winsor, *The Westward Movement* (Boston, 1897), p. 216.

[23] Edward Channing, *History of the United States* (New York, 1910), II, 603.

[24] Antonio Ferrer del Rio, "El Conde de Aranda. Su dictamen sobre la America Española," *Revista Española de Ambos Mundos* (Madrid), III (May, 1855). In this extended article Ferrer del Rio maintains, rather unconvincingly, that the memoir is not authentic. He bases his contention on the assertion that it is inconsistent with other known statements of Aranda before and after this time. He quotes (in Spanish, p. 567) from the memoir as he finds it printed (in French) in Muriel's translation of William Coxe, *Spain under the Bourbons*. The memoir is not printed in Coxe's book, but Muriel's edition contains additional material and presents the Aranda document from the copy which was in the papers of the Duke of San Fernando.

[25] *Cambridge Modern History* (Cambridge, 1910), XII, 691. This is quoted without reference to any source, but is in accord with the Spanish text presented by Ferrer del Rio. See also a version of the "colossus" paragraph in Justin Winsor, *Narrative and Critical History of America* (Boston, 1888), VII, 152 fn., also quoted without reference. The differences between Winsor's text and the one in the *Cambridge Modern History* arise because the former selects some additional sentences, leaves out various phrases, and combines the statement into a continuous quotation without the use of omission marks. All his phrases may be found in the Ferrer del Rio extract.

[26] Charles Gayarré, *History of Louisiana* (New Orleans, 1885), III, 216–217.

[27] James A. Robertson, *Louisiana under the Rule of Spain, France, and the United States, 1785–1807* (Cleveland, 1911), I, 297.

[28] *Ibid.*, p. 298.

[29] Jedidiah Morse, *The American Geography* (Elizabethtown, N. J., 1789), pp. 468–469.

[30] Gilbert Imlay, *A Topographical Description of the Western Territory of North America* (London, 1792), p. vii.

[31] *Ibid.*, p. 107.

[32] *Ibid.*, p. 108.

[33] *Ibid.* (3d ed., 1797), p. 76 fn. The Rev. Manassah Cutler, in 1787,

discussing the westward expansion of the republic, maintained that the national capital would be moved to the Ohio River. William F. and Julia P. Cutler, *Life, Journals, and Correspondence of Rev. Manassah Cutler* (Cincinnati, 1888), II, 405–406.

[34] Paul Leicester Ford (ed.), *Writings of Jefferson* (New York, 1892–1899), II, 92–93.

[35] Thomas Jefferson to George Rogers Clark, December 4, 1783, in Reuben G. Thwaites (ed.), *Original Journals of the Lewis and Clark Expedition, 1804–1806* (New York, 1905), VII, 193.

[36] Ford, *Writings of Jefferson*, III, 400–402; IV, 363–364, 391, 392, 451; V, 63.

[37] Thomas Jefferson to Archibald Stuart, January 25, 1786, *ibid.,* IV, 188–189.

[38] *Ibid.,* p. 180.

[39] The Jefferson letters with regard to John Ledyard's schemes are collected in Thwaites, *Original Journals of the Lewis and Clark Expedition*, VIII, 195–196.

[40] Ford, *Writings of Jefferson,* V, 218–221.

[41] *Ibid.,* p. 229.

[42] *Ibid.,* VIII, 105.

[43] *American State Papers* (Foreign Relations), II, 525–526.

[44] Thwaites, *Original Journals of the Lewis and Clark Expedition,* VII, 209.

[45] Jefferson to John C. Breckenridge, August 12, 1803, in Ford, *Writings of Jefferson*, VIII, 243.

THE INTRIGUES OF DR.
JAMES O'FALLON

—◦⋘⋙◦—

SIDE BY SIDE with the machinations of James
Wilkinson in the unquiet region of the trans-Allegheny were the intrigues of a number of lesser characters. Usually these plotters helped spin the intricate
web that radiated from the arch-conspirator in Frank-
fort, or united their minor strands with the various
ramifications of his major designs. Sometimes they in-
terfered with the pattern he had in mind and straightway found themselves entangled in the stuff they were
weaving. Notable among these contemporaries was
Dr. James O'Fallon.

This curious Irish adventurer, friend of Tom Paine
and Anthony Wayne, and brother-in-law of George
Rogers Clark, spent twenty hectic years in America and
in that time played many roles. In 1776 he was jailed
as a man dangerous to the patriotic cause. In 1777 he
was a captain of cavalry, and in 1779 a senior surgeon
in the revolutionary service. In 1783 and 1784 he was
a fanatical antiloyalist; in 1788 he sought the privilege
of colonizing Irish Catholics in Spanish East Florida;
in the early 1790's he was the central figure in the west-

ern intrigues over the Yazoo lands, and the associate of George Rogers Clark in Genêt's threatened attack upon Louisiana.

But he was never a successful adventurer. The Yazoo Company failed to support him, Kentucky friends deserted him, Wilkinson betrayed him, the President of the United States denounced him in a proclamation, the King of Spain issued orders for his arrest, he came to blows with George Rogers Clark, his wife left him, and early in 1794 he died with no obituary in the newspapers and apparently little mourning over his departure.

James O'Fallon, or Fallon as he was known throughout most of his life, was born on March 11, 1749, in county Roscommon, Ireland. Practically the only source of information in regard to his early life is a sketch given to Lyman Draper by his son, John O'Fallon.[1] John was but two years old when his father died, and the document bears all the earmarks of James O'Fallon's own preparation. Parents of means gave him the advantage of travel on the Continent and two years of medical study at the University of Edinburgh. He did not graduate from the University,[2] but, having somewhere acquired the title of doctor, he set out in 1774 for the British colonies in America, moved, so the account runs, by the desire to join a revolt which seemed imminent. "The strong spirit of freedom was already in James, and, (as a *genuine* Irishman) an hereditary aversion to British oppression."[3]

---

[1] For notes see pages 119–129.

After being shipwrecked, he landed on the coast of North Carolina and settled for the practice of his profession in the town of Wilmington. Here he was shortly on the best of terms with the leading families of the region, including (despite his "hereditary aversion") the British Governor, Josiah Martin. But "he no sooner breathed the American air," writes his inspired chronicler, "than he perceived, the strong impulses of liberty and the desire of humbling the ancient oppressor of his native country and family, throbbing within him."[4] He broke—we are told—with the British Governor and was imprisoned for attacking him in verse and prose. Whereupon there came to his rescue county militia to the number of 800 men who carried him out of prison into the streets in an armchair on their heads, and created such a patriotic tumult that the Governor was forthwith exiled to a King's ship in the river.[5]

This makes a pretty story, but the contemporary documents printed in the *North Carolina Colonial Records* give quite a different version. The minutes of the Committee of Safety of Wilmington for January 15, 1776, show that body to have ordered Fallon into custody in the guardhouse because he had written a paper which was put up to public view under the courthouse. It was signed "A Lawyer" and was addressed "To those who have a true sense of distributive justice and untrammeled liberty, residents of the borough of Wilmington." The paper was said to contain "many false and scandalous reflections on this committee, tending to inflame the minds of the people; to create division and dissention amongst us by destroying that unanimity so essentially necessary to our mutual defence; and also containing an illiberal and groundless charge against a respectable gentleman deservedly high in office in this colony."[6]

A few days later, Colonel Moore reported that he considered "Dr Fallon to be an insinuating and dangerous person among the soldiers and that he can not, without injuring the common cause and running the risk of the public safety any longer keep the said Fallon in the Guard House." So the Committee of Safety ordered him transferred to the common jail.[7] In jail the irrepressible Doctor continued the use of his pen "to repeat and justify his offences," whereat the Committee forbade him all visitors[8] and refused his request for a copy of the paper signed "A Lawyer" which had stirred up all the trouble.[9]

Whatever may have been the contents of this paper, and whatever the sentiments which Colonel Moore deemed so injurious to the common cause, there is no room for doubt that ultimately Fallon joined the revolutionary forces. His own sketch tells of his gallant service in the engagement at Moore's Bridge, and credits him with organizing thereafter a hundred Irishmen from the western part of North Carolina into a company which was attached to a Georgia battalion and ordered into Pennsylvania.[10]

His professional training, however, led to his assign-

ment to the medical service and he became a surgeon
in the Pennsylvania Line.[11] In April, 1779, he wrote to
Dr. Thomas Burke, later Governor of North Carolina,
from Fishkill, New York, where he was then senior surgeon in the hospital.[12] This letter gives evidence of previous service of a similar nature in Connecticut. In the
later years of the war, he appears to have been again
in Pennsylvania.[13] The Continental Congress, in January, 1782, recommended Fallon and other surgeons of
the general hospitals to the state of Pennsylvania for
pay,[14] and Pennsylvania took favorable action in 1784.[15]

At the close of the war, according to Fallon's own
narrative, "in company with his friend Major Pierce
Butler, Mrs. Butler, and Comodore Alexander Gillon,
he set out for Charleston in South Carolina, and there
settled in extensive practice."[16] His trail may thereafter
be picked up in the files of the Charleston newspapers
and in the correspondence of Archibald Maclaine of
Wilmington, North Carolina, with George Hooper of
Charleston. Maclaine had been a member of the Wilmington Committee of Safety at the time of Fallon's
incarceration in 1776.

"I am sorry," Maclaine wrote, early in 1783, "that my
want of leisure will not permit me to give you the history (as far as I am acquainted with it) of the life and
adventures of the *divine-physical* gentlemen to whom
you allude. This is the epithet bestowed upon him by
his cousin, Hugh Kelly of London, whom he took in
for a considerable sum, at the very time he was deter-

mined on his voyage to our continent. As soon as my time will permit, I will help you out. I owe the scoundrel something on my own account."[17]

Fallon was soon in the thick of a radical, antiloyalist movement, led by Alexander Gillon, the "Comodore" with whom he had left Philadelphia.[18] A club known as the "Smoking Society," converted into the "Marine Anti-Britannic Society," became the vehicle of their activity, with Gillon as president and Fallon as secretary; and in the columns of the Charleston newspapers thereafter appear frequent communications from "James Fallon, Secretary," calling meetings, reporting rules and resolutions, and presenting letters to editors.[19]

The political feeling in the city was bitter, and frequent attacks were made upon the leaders. In the *South Carolina Gazette and General Advertiser*[20] appears a long letter from "A Steady and Open Republican" which includes a statement to the effect that "Mr. *Official* Secretary has declared, that, like another Pompey, at a stamp of his foot, he could start up 500 men."[21] The remark is quite in key with many of the later pronouncements of the voluble Doctor.

The letters of Maclaine, a man of prominence in his state and in the patriotic cause, contain many references to Fallon. He writes of protested notes of Fallon's to the extent of £200 sterling, reiterates the charge that the Doctor came to America on money euchred out of his lame cousin, Hugh Kelly, and states that General Greene is very solicitous to have authenticated the basis of this charge.[22] But the antiloyal agitation died out in 1785,[23] and in the discussion of new issues to which the parties turned Fallon does not appear to have taken a conspicuous part.

A distinctly new phase of Fallon's career began in the latter part of the 1780's when he opened negotiations with Spanish officials. In this new capacity we find him parading under a slightly different name, and henceforth to the end of his days he is known under the more high-sounding cognomen of O'Fallon.[24] In May, 1788, he wrote to Don Diego de Gardoqui, Spanish chargé d'affaires in New York, a letter accompanied by a long document outlining an ambitious scheme for the colonization of the northern part of East Florida.[25] In the letter itself he dwelt at great length upon the international situation, stressing the danger to Spain in America from two principal agencies: the growing power of the United States, and the machinations of Great Britain. He charged England with definitely manipulating the treaty of peace in 1783 so as to break the harmony between the United States and the two Bourbon nations. The cession of the land beyond the Alleghenies as far south as the thirty-first parallel, and the arrangement for the common enjoyment of the free navigation of the Mississippi, were, according to O'Fallon, definitely for the purpose of sowing seeds of discord between the United States and Spain, and indirectly of bringing about the destruction of the alliance with France. This being accomplished, England would make an alliance of her own, either with the United States as a whole or with detached and independent states formed by the settlers on the "western waters." This menace to the Spanish provinces would have to be met soon.

The growing strength of the United States, greatly increased by the new Constitution, would threaten the Floridas and New Orleans, which the Americans coveted. All these dangers, O'Fallon maintained, made action by Spain imperative and to that end he presented his colonization scheme, to be coupled with certain "political measures." He remarked that for him to present these political measures in his letter would be imprudent; but his reference to the need of political relations with the Americans residing on the "western waters," and his mention of proposals he had received from Kentucky and Franklin, make it seem probable that he had in mind capitalization by Spain of the separatist tendency of the trans-Allegheny West.

He closed his letter with an attempt to strengthen his position by emphasizing the Spanish origin of his family and the services his kinsmen had rendered on behalf of Spain. He generously offered to come to New York or even to go to Madrid to discuss the plan of colonization, provided only that his expenses were paid.

The document which accompanied his letter and presented the actual scheme of colonization contained many thousand words, but it can be summed up briefly.

He proposed that the Spanish government turn over to him a tract of land across the northern margin of East Florida, sufficient to give 857 acres each to 5,000 heads of families whom he would colonize in the district during a period of seven years. He stipulated that he might admit, as associates, not more than five other persons, who would form with him a company for the better execution of his project. He and his associates would become citizens of Spain and the colonists would be required to take an oath of allegiance to the Spanish Crown. The subjects whom O'Fallon planned to collect were all to be Catholic and would be mostly Irishmen, although he expected during the seven years of recruiting to travel over America, Ireland, Great Britain, Flanders, France, Germany, and Holland in search of the best material. He suggested that he receive for his work an annual salary of a thousand guineas, plus five hundred more for traveling expenses—a sum small, he remarked, in comparison with his yearly income as a physician in Charleston. There would be certain expenses to the Crown for the transportation of colonists to East Florida, but O'Fallon estimated that the entire cost of the project during the seven-year period would not be more than £250,000, and he waxed eloquent over the 20,000 loyal souls whom he could so easily gather and set up as a rampart against American aggression or English intrigue. A characteristic touch appears in O'Fallon's argument, that the scheme would not only be a project for a valuable colony but would

also give him the opportunity while traveling abroad
to ferret out secrets and pick up information as to the
designs of foreign cabinets which might affect the in-
tests of the Spanish Crown, which employed him.

Gardoqui sent the letter and document on to Floridablanca in Madrid, saying that, according to report,
O'Fallon was a restless and turbulent adventurer.
Nevertheless, he had thought it wise to answer him
courteously, promising him that his project would be
given consideration and the result communicated to
him.[26] This was probably the end of the matter, although O'Fallon later claimed to have carried on extensive relations with Gardoqui, as a colonizer and as a
spy upon British and American activities.[27]

The trans-Allegheny region, however, offered at this
time the best field for intrigue. Wilkinson's successful
trip to New Orleans in 1787 had no doubt influenced
the scheme of O'Fallon in East Florida as it did the
projects of George Morgan, George Rogers Clark, and
others in various parts of the West.[28] The region about
the mouth of the Yazoo River offered particularly strategic attractions, and Wilkinson himself had written to
Gardoqui asking for a colonial concession at this point
where he, together with Innes, Sebastian, Dunn, and
Brown, might find refuge under Spanish authority in
time of need.[29]

In Charleston, South Carolina, three men of influence, Alexander Moultrie, William Clay Snipes, and
Isaac Huger, were planning bold deeds in the realm

of western real estate. Associated with them was a
Georgian adventurer, Thomas Washington, whose real
name is said to have been Thomas Walsh, and who a
few years later was hanged in Charleston for counterfeiting.[30] This group of four men acquired a grant of
land in the Yazoo country from the Choctaws, organized
the South Carolina Yazoo Company, and began vigorous action for a colony.[31]

In 1789 they deputized Captain John Holder to proceed with supplies to the region, and secured the co-
operation of John Cape, a Kentuckian, with respect
to Indian affairs. Meanwhile they began a movement
to get a grant from the state of Georgia. In September
and October they wrote enthusiastic letters to Holder
and Cape assuring them that the succes of the legisla-
tive program was no longer in doubt and urging them
to take instant possession, establish friendly relations
with the Indians, and make overtures to the Spanish
officials. The implication of an independent state is
unmistakable in these letters.[32]

This correspondence came into the hands of James
Wilkinson, who was of course greatly interested. Here
was a well-backed project aimed at the very region in
which he and his Kentucky friends had hoped to settle.
He passed the letters on to Estevan Miró, Spanish Governor at New Orleans, with the characteristic remark
that both Holder and Cape were dependent upon him
and were inconsequential creatures from whom he did
not anticipate trouble.[33] He reported further that he

had written to Moultrie and his associates giving advice and suggesting that he act as their agent.[34] He thus hoped to bring about, he said, the attachment of the new state to the domains of Spain.

In the meantime the Georgia legislature had made grants of land on the Mississippi to three companies, the Virginia Company, the Tennessee Company, and the South Carolina Yazoo Company. The last, reorganized and enlarged into a company with twenty shares, chose Alexander Moultrie as director and Dr. James O'Fallon as general agent.[35] O'Fallon was given instructions to proceed to Kentucky, get an accounting of goods from Holder, recruit and initiate the colony at the mouth of the Yazoo, conciliate the Indians, and visit New Orleans for the purpose of establishing relations with the Spanish Governor. He was to appoint agents, subordinate to himself, for Kentucky and the Yazoo country, and also keep an agent among the Choctaws. These instructions, signed by Moultrie on March 9, 1790, make no reference to the United States government nor to the relations of the colony thereto. On the other hand, they include no statement which could be said clearly to indicate separatism, as did the letters written by the members of the company to Holder and Cape in the preceding year. Additional secret instructions were issued to O'Fallon, but these have not been found.[36]

O'Fallon set out at once, and after stopping on the way to talk with leaders in South and North Carolina,

and at Jonesboro to concert with John Sevier, who had
asked to join the company, he arrived at Lexington on
April 27.[37] In Kentucky he immediately came in touch
with Wilkinson, to whom he brought a letter from
Moultrie thanking him for his offer of services as general agent. Although O'Fallon had been given that
position, the company welcomed the coöperation of
Wilkinson and offered him a share in the enterprise.[38]

O'Fallon was not a wholly astute person and probably had little idea of the man with whom he now associated. Wary at first, he soon came to repose complete
confidence in Wilkinson. But Wilkinson was merely
following the policy of controlling his competitor. Furthermore, with the waning of his hopes for an independent Kentucky, the new project was welcome
because it gave him a means by which he could exact
pay from Spain for protecting Spanish interests. He continued to inform Miró of every move. For the time being he supported O'Fallon and, though criticizing him
somewhat as a light and vain personage, reported him
to Miró as a real and useful friend of Spain.[39] About the
time O'Fallon arrived in Kentucky, Miró, alarmed at
Wilkinson's account of the project of the South Carolina Company, wrote to the General stating unequivo-
cally that the Indian grant was unlawful, that the grant
from Georgia was for territory belonging to Spain, and
that any attempt to settle in the Yazoo country would
be forcibly resisted.[40]

In Kentucky O'Fallon began at once the collection

of goods from Holder and the organization of his colonial venture. He also planned for a visit to New Orleans. Two letters to Miró exhibit his ideas. One was written May 24, 1790. He was coming down to New Orleans in June to lay his credentials and plans before the Governor. The colony was to be independent of the United States, ready to form a close alliance with Spain and to serve as a rampart for the protection of her frontier provinces. To this initial organization all the territory west of the Alleghenies would gravitate, renouncing in turn their allegiance to the Union. The letter was couched in extravagant terms, warmly expounding his affection for Spain.[41]

The second letter, written July 16, 1790, was still more remarkable. By this time he had learned from Wilkinson of Miró's plan of resistance to the colonial establishment and he evidently thought that such a statement of policy must be countered by a threat. So, while reiterating his allegiance to the Spanish nation and extolling the advantages to Spain of such a union, he asked, rather baldly, what would happen if Miró refused to allow such an establishment. No doubts existed in his mind that the company would prosecute its enterprise in any event, systematically and, if necessary, with the use of force. In case of such hostilities he, O'Fallon, must resign his agency (being wholly devoted to Spain), and another less friendly agent would be in charge. Furthermore, the company, if attacked by Spain or the Indians, would (despite their separatist plans) call upon Congress for help, which the United States government, in his opinion, could not refuse. Thus would be reopened the old differences between the two countries involving boundaries and the use of the Mississippi River, and these differences the Kentuckians and Frankliners, galled by restrictions at New Orleans, would soon bring to an issue.

O'Fallon thought it wise to make the most of the military preparations. There were already engaged from the Carolinas and Georgia and Franklin "from three to five thousand well armed Men, without the incumbrance of Females, or Children," who would move out with the first establishment. This number did not include those who would come from Kentucky or the forces sent by the other land companies. The colonists were to meet at the Long Island of Holston River, whence boats would take them down the Tennessee, Ohio, and Mississippi rivers to the Yazoo. They planned to arrive with strength superior to any attack. They were to be arranged by companies in military townships with 100 fighting men in each. The companies were to be grouped in battalions, battalions in brigades, and the whole subjected to rigid military discipline. In addition to this militia, there would be a standing force of three cavalry companies and 400 infantrymen always on duty.

This threatening array, led by an agent less sympathetic than O'Fallon, would bode ill for Spain. To put it in O'Fallon's weird metaphor, it "may bring a *Fire-*

brand to your Door, which however effectually you may be enabled to circumscribe its blaze for a time, may at length throw such a spark into the combustibles which daily accumulate within the Bowells of these States, as would eventually plunge this Empire and your's into a general combustion."[42]

The letter of May 24 put Miró in a reflective mood and he wrote to the Spanish Minister, stating the arguments pro and con, but stressing the theory that Spain should found its own colonies. He had taken the precaution, he said, to secure the promise of the Indians to attack any Americans who came upon their lands, and as for O'Fallon, he would so manage him as to keep him hopeful until he received further instructions from Spain.[43] As late as September 20, Miró expressed himself to Wilkinson as eagerly awaiting the arrival of O'Fallon, in order that he might direct the project toward the ends which he deemed the most useful to his king.[44] Perhaps Miró had in mind the possibility which he had mentioned to Valdez, of controlling the colony by accepting immigrants who would come as subjects of Spain. He made no reference to O'Fallon's letter of July 16, and probably had not yet received it. Before the end of the month, however, this document had reached him and caused him considerable disturbance of mind. Wilkinson's injunction to be tranquil and trust him for news did not comport well with O'Fallon's story of such extensive military preparations.[45]

But Miró answered O'Fallon suavely and cordially.

It was with great satisfaction that he observed the friendship which O'Fallon professed for Spain, and the Doctor's relations with Wilkinson added to the favorable impression. He had written to the Court about his plans and hoped for flattering results. With many compliments he expressed the hope that O'Fallon would soon make the trip to New Orleans. When he arrived at Bayou Pierre, Colonel Bruin would give him a passport, at Natchez he would receive a convincing welcome, and at New Orleans he would find in Miró himself a friend favorably disposed to the matter in question. This letter seems not to have reached O'Fallon, who had to rely upon indirect evidence as to Miró's reception of his proposal.[46]

Meanwhile O'Fallon was very busy in Kentucky. His visit to New Orleans was postponed from time to time, though his military preparations went on apace. On September 16, 1790, a battalion of about 650 men was enrolled, with John Holder as its colonel and commander. It consisted of a troop of cavalry, a company of artillery, and eight companies of riflemen. O'Fallon, on behalf of the South Carolina Yazoo Company, signed articles of contract making detailed provisions for the military organization. He promised, furthermore, to every woman "married or marriageable" who should accompany the troops to the settlement, a hundred acres of land, and "as a bounty of encouragement to female adventurers . . . five hundred acres of land to the first woman who shall land there; and five hundred more to her who shall bring forth in it the first live child, bastard or legitimate."[47]

O'Fallon kept the company in Charleston apprised of his doings during the summer and fall of 1790. He reported progress with Holder, with the Choctaws, with the Spanish Governor, and with his military arrangements. The proprietors were greatly pleased and on September 5 wrote to the General Agent signifying their entire approbation.[48] On the same day Alexander Moultrie wrote to Wilkinson telling of his enthusiasm over O'Fallon's activities and his pleasure at the assistance which Wilkinson was giving him.[49] Wilkinson replied assuring Moultrie that he would coöperate with O'Fallon in every way possible.[50]

Early in October O'Fallon gave the company a full account of his military organization.[51] A fortnight later he reported his battalion complete and his departure imminent.[52] On November 6, he had not yet gone down to the Yazoo country but sent word that his "clerk at New Orleans, Mr. Nolan" had assured him that no opposition would now be made to the settlement either by Spaniards or Indians. Within five or six days the first detachment of 300 men would set out. He himself would soon follow them, and 300 more troops and about 600 families would go down the river in February. "Everything as yet has favored me. I stay here that I may leave nothing of moment to chance. Sevier is jealous; he is of great moment to our interests. Why have you not written to him?"[53] After this letter the company for several months did not hear from its agent.

The fall days of 1790 were not occupied entirely with military affairs. O'Fallon turned his attention seriously to the task of advertising the colony. There appeared in the *Kentucky Gazette* a Philadelphia news item headed: "Extract of a letter from a gentleman in Lexington, (Kentucky.) to his friend in this City."[54] The letter was dated October 20, 1790, and was evidently written by O'Fallon. He described enthusiastically the soil, products, and possibilities of the new colony, and announced progress and plans far ahead of those he had reported to the company. A hundred families had been sent down in June by the General Agent, by whose efforts the Indians and Spaniards were reconciled to the enterprise, and O'Fallon himself was to set out immediately with his battalion. General Scott of Kentucky was to take 500 families with him.[55] Wilkinson was to follow with 1,000 fighting men and their families by Christmas, and General Sevier was to take down a similar number. General McDowell would accompany the Frankliners from Long Island on the Holston with 300 from the back parts of North Carolina. Two hundred were to come from Cumberland, and great numbers from the country of Alexander McGillivray, who was claimed a member of the company. This was the glowing prospect on October 20, 1790. It scarcely needs to be observed that if O'Fallon could have achieved such a combination of leaders, troops, and colonists, he would have had no further necessity of conciliating the Spaniards, and the people on the "western waters" could have dictated their own terms as to the possession of the trans-Allegheny region and the use of the Mississippi River.

But two such men as Wilkinson and O'Fallon could hardly work long in unison. Each, intent upon his own ends, accepted the other's friendship merely for selfish reasons. Both spoke often and loudly of honor, but neither one possessed any. Each was ready to desert or betray when it suited him. On the day that the enthusiastic prospectus of the colony was penned, Wilkinson had assured Moultrie of his coöperation with O'Fallon. On November 4, according to his own story, he wrote to Moultrie severing his connection with the company and saying merely that O'Fallon had departed so far from his original plans that as a man of honor he could no longer have dealings with him. In December he wrote to Miró that he had discovered that O'Fallon was "a man destitute of sincerity or good faith" whose plan was to use his military power to gain forcible possession of Walnut Hills at the mouth of the Yazoo, and that without openly breaking with O'Fallon he had begun to undermine him.[56]

Several months later Wilkinson gave Miró a full account of the means he had taken to ruin his associate.[57] He reported that O'Fallon's plan to seize Walnut Hills was predicated upon the belief that Miró would not venture to oppose him because—war with England being apparently imminent on account of the Nootka Sound affair—the Governor would be afraid of finding himself between two fires. Wilkinson made the most of the situation. He described to Miró how, enraged though he was at O'Fallon's breach of faith and honor, he had preserved his composure and hidden his wrath but was determined to destroy the Doctor's nefarious designs. He struck secretly at O'Fallon's base of supplies. The Agent had been drawing on the company to pay for materials in Kentucky. Wilkinson now sent a friend, Captain Manning, to South Carolina to insinuate to the company the misuse of funds by O'Fallon and a general incompetence that was bringing the project into ruin. By this means Wilkinson caused one of O'Fallon's drafts on the company to be protested. Meantime he had turned his attention to O'Fallon's battalion and succeeded, so he said, in reducing it from 500 to 50 men. When he wrote to Miró in March, 1791, he recorded the opinion that "the grand project will die a natural death and pass away without convulsions."[58]

Turning to the other intriguer, we find that as early as September, 1790, O'Fallon, who dearly loved a lengthy document, wrote a letter of about thirty pages to the President of the United States. Probably this was an attempt to placate Washington, who, fearing the possible effect of the land operations upon Indian affairs, had issued a proclamation in August, 1790, requiring obedience to the Indian treaties and regulations.[59]

O'Fallon's letter outlined, with discretion, the plans
of his company and asked the consent of the government of the United States to their establishment, re-
marking, however, that they were able and determined
in any case to carry out the project. Then (according
to evidence presented by Wilkinson) he gave full sweep
to his pen and communicated in detail the separatist
tendencies of various westerners. Although he did not
name Wilkinson, he so vividly described him that there
was no mistaking his identity, told of his employment
by Spain for the separation of Kentucky from the
Union, and disclosed the contents of Wilkinson's correspondence with Spanish officials. He then suggested
that he could secure important information if employed by Washington as a secret agent and spy. The
paragraphs of the letter which contained the alleged
betrayal of the Kentucky leaders are reported to us only
in the documents forwarded to Miró by Wilkinson,
and may have been an interpolation on the part of that
resourceful plotter. But they were not out of key with
the character of O'Fallon. The letter had apparently
no immediate reaction, though it brought very definite
results a few months later.[60]

Through the winter, O'Fallon proceeded with his
operations in Kentucky and continued his correspondence with the Spanish Governor. There was a marked
change, however, in his affairs. He made friends with
George Rogers Clark, Wilkinson's military rival, and
in November, 1790, secured Clark's assent to command

the troops organized for the Yazoo venture.[61] This shift
from Wilkinson to Clark is clearly reflected in his letters. Writing to Miró in December from the residence
of General Clark, he reaffirmed his strong attachment
to Spain and his idea of an independent Trans-Allegheny, but there was a new note of truculence in his
lines and no longer any flattering words for Wilkinson.
In fact the letter was evidently called forth by mistrust
of Wilkinson and by rumors of Spanish hostility, and
it therefore teemed with threats of military invasion
and English or American coalition.

The prospect of war between Spain and England
and the treaty of McGillivray with the United States
were bogies which he now used to advantage. Miró
must know, he remarked, that other European alliances
could have been easily obtained if Spain had not been
preferred. The United States, as well, knew the strategic advantages and dangers of the company's location; and President Washington, he said, had recently
written to the company offering the support of the
American forces, and money for the expenses of the
battalion, and expressing the desire that the General
Agent give him regular information as to the doings
of the Spaniards and Indians. The company, however,
were merely holding this offer as a last resort.

O'Fallon now came to the real point of his letter. He
informed Miró that a declaration had been made before Colonel Marshall, reporting the Spanish Governor
as inciting the Indians against the colony. He also un-

derstood that the deposition charged Wilkinson and
Sebastian with implication in the plot and named these
two along with Innes and Brown as holding Spanish
commissions. Such rumors and declarations, he said,
might ruin "poor Wilkinson" since Marshall had sent
the document on to Washington. As for the story of pre-
arranged assault upon the colony, O'Fallon said he had
not credited it or he would not now be writing and
renewing his sentiments of friendship. He did believe
and fear the activities of Secretaries Knox and Hamilton, who were negotiating with Great Britain and
planning for posts in the Yazoo country. It was because
of this danger to Spain and to his colony that he was
making such great military preparations.

In case of danger General Clark would command his
troops. Clark, he said, was a friend of Spain and his
agent for Kentucky, as Sevier was for Franklin and
James Robertson for Cumberland. O'Fallon claimed, as
one of the proprietors of the company, Alexander Mc-
Gillivray,[62] and if this Creek chieftain's hereditary foes,
the Choctaws, should make any hostile move, armed
forces would be led through the Creek country to the
colony by William Moultrie, ex-Governor of South
Carolina, General Huger, General Marion, General
McDowell, General McIntosh, Governor Telfair of
Georgia, and others of the proprietors. O'Fallon observed, however, that the company expected Miró to
prove his good will by influencing the Choctaws and
Chickasaws to be favorable to the colony. Otherwise

the sword must be unsheathed and the Yazoo Company would be found to have friends in both Indian nations. Did Miró wish to lose the friendship of a colony that could choose as its allies America, England, or the Indians?[63]

The menacing tone of the letter alarmed the Spanish government, but it did not bring the result which O'Fallon wished. The true explanation of the letter lay in the reference to Miró's instigation of the Indians. This was what O'Fallon deeply feared, for it presented a fatal obstacle to his plans just when his project was reaching a climax. His last resort was always to threats, and by this means he now hoped to prevent Miró from making trouble for him with the Choctaws and Chickasaws. This accounts for the continuation of his correspondence with Miró long after he must have seen the futility of expecting a welcome for his colony from the Spanish government.

After a trip to Franklin and Cumberland to visit friends, O'Fallon wrote to Miró in January, 1791, telling of his enthusiasm over the thousands who were coming to join his colony from all the Atlantic states. But he now threw pretense aside, charged Miró directly with inciting the Indians, and urged him to recall his instructions to them. His letter was a mixture of boasting, pleading, and threatening. The company preferred Spain as an ally, but if Miró should reject such overtures they would join Great Britain, with whom negotiations had been broached through Lord Dorchester.

If the Indians should molest the colony, O'Fallon
would hold Miró as directly responsible and would attack the Spanish towns from St. Louis to New Orleans,
and Mobile and Pensacola as well. If, on the other
hand, the Spanish Governor should be disposed to be
friendly and should reconcile and calm the Indians instead of exciting them, he would give his word of honor
that Miró would never have a better ally. The numbers and equipment of his forces were such that the
Choctaws and Chickasaws would not even be "a light
breakfast" for them; but he implored Miró to tran-
quillize them before his arrival, and ended by begging
him "in the name of God" to send him an express immediately.[64] Another letter in February made much of
an English alliance, McGillivray's power with the Indians, and his own thousands of soldiers, and pleaded
with Miró to accept the colony as an ally, quiet the Indian tribes, and thus avoid war. He had now postponed
his trip down the river till autumn.[65] Miró responded
to the two letters in March. He denied the charge of
inciting the Indians against the colony, held out hope
of an alliance, and urged the General Agent to make his
long-deferred visit to New Orleans.[66]

It seems obvious that O'Fallon had, in spite of his
protestations, abandoned his first hope of a friendly
alliance with Spain, and was now intent on a forcible
seizure on behalf of his company, if the Indian danger
could be removed. The international situation presented England as a possibly ally, and O'Fallon was

perhaps optimistic enough to hope that if all else failed he might fall back on the support of the United States. At all events, threats of such alliances might scare the Spanish out of intrigues with the Indians.

An event occurring in February, 1791, probably had an influence in postponing O'Fallon's departure for the Yazoo country. In the latter part of the month he was married to Frances Clark, the younger sister of George Rogers Clark.[67] A prenuptial contract signed on February 21 binds O'Fallon in the sum of £5,000 sterling, to be paid to his wife on the occasion of his death.[68] These appear to have been the halcyon days of James O'Fallon. Although he had lost the support of Wilkinson, he was doubly bound now to the hero of the Revolution in the West. And the prenuptial contract deals fluently with the Doctor's mansion house and plantation, his slaves, his stock, and his furniture.

In the month before his marriage he wrote out a set of directions for the preservation of the health of his prospective father-in-law and mother-in-law, covering the questions of clothing, habits, and diet. He recommended that Mr. Clark procure "two pairs of Flannel drawers, and as many pair of Flannel shirts. The former ought to be of red, or scarlet colour, on account of the Dye extracted from the cutcheoneel animal, which is peculiarly salutary against all Pains in the Hips, and inferior joints. The latter may be white; as being the more absorbent, and the more productive of a gentle Perspiration." He prescribed "calomile" for the "colicky complaints of the nervous kind, to which you have been so addicted." To Mrs. Clark he gave somewhat similar advice, closing by saying "a cheerful Heart, Temper, and Disposition ... is one of the best Preventatives against your, and, indeed, against every Disease."[69]

Kindly concern for his wife's future finances and for her parents' physical welfare paralleled his engrossing task of gathering men and supplies and concerting military plans with George Rogers Clark. Thus he spent the first two months of the year 1791. But before his honeymoon was over the collapse of his enterprise was well under way. In the Senate of the United States, on January 24, 1791, O'Fallon's letter of the preceding September was read—a "volume of a letter," one of the Senators, William Maclay, called it in his *Journal*.[70] President Washington had submitted the document to the Senate for consideration along with a report by the Secretary of War "relative to the frontiers."[71] John Brown, Congressman from the district of Kentucky, sent a description of it to his friend Wilkinson, and Wilkinson sent on to Miró a copy of Brown's letter.[72] If this copy is to be trusted, O'Fallon's epistle contained an exposure of Kentucky separatist leaders and of Wilkinson in particular. On the strength of this asserted attack, Wilkinson appealed to Miró for help. He reminded the Spanish Governor of O'Fallon's letter of the preceding July 16, with its extravagant praise for Spain and its contempt for the United States, and asked Miró to send him the original of the Doctor's letter that he might use it as undeniable evidence of O'Fallon's duplicity.[73]

Miró was unwilling to comply with this request until he should obtain authority from his superiors.[74] But long before Wilkinson had time even to get a reply from the Governor, swift-moving events impelled him to take action. On the same day that Wilkinson wrote his letter to Miró—March 19—the consideration by the United States government of the threatening affairs on the frontier reached a culmination. Washington issued a proclamation warning the West against O'Fallon,[75] and orders were sent to the Attorney of the District of Kentucky to proceed against the Doctor.[76] Wilkinson undoubtedly received immediate if not advance notice of this, and acted at once. He resorted to the well-worn device of the anonymous letter as a means of scaring and getting rid of O'Fallon. On the 30th of March he sent him the following note:

Sir: The Heavens are unpropitious to you, & the affairs of man depend so much upon casualty, that Genius or Education availeth naught:—by a gentleman just arrived from Philadelphia by way of PittsBurgh, I am confidentially informed, the sec[ty]. of the Treasury has secretly assured Him that whilst the Congress was deliberateing on a Letter of yours to the President of the 30th Sept[r]. a Letter of the 16th July, said to be written by you to the Gov[nr]. of N Orleans, was, to the astonishment of all, introduced thro the same Channel to the same Body; and that in consequence thereof, the Congress had directed the President, to issue a special Warrant, under the great seal of the Union, for your apprehension, with orders that you should be carried forward to the seat of the Gen[l]. Government as a conspirator & that Mr. John Brown, who may be momently expected to arrive here, was commissioned for the express purpose, of carrying this mandate into execution; My friendship for you induces me to give you this advice, that you may without a moments delay, secure a retreat to some place of safety, until the annimossity of the moment may subside, or blow over; excuse a fictitious hand & want of signature; times are ticklish, &, tho desirous to serve, to assist, & to save you, I cannot commit myself to hazard this goes by an Indirect, but I trust an expiditious conveyance—Adieu[77]

The statement that both letters were read is not supported by the record, and Wilkinson probably twisted the facts with the idea of making the situation seem more desperate to O'Fallon. We have, in a letter to Miró, Wilkinson's own account of the writing of the anonymous communication. ". . . To hang up this son of Lucifer on the tenterhooks of apprehension & dismay, & if possible to force him into your government, I have written him an anonymous letter, in a disguised hand, of which the enclosed is a copy."[78]

O'Fallon does not appear to have fled from Kentucky, nor was he arrested. It is not improbable that Wilkinson's desire to drive him out of the country was based upon a fear that if O'Fallon should be arrested by United States officials his disclosures might be unfortunate for Wilkinson and his associates. The Attorney of the District of Kentucky, to whom was given the responsibility of proceeding against O'Fallon, was

George Nicholas, a friend of Wilkinson, and this may account for the failure of the hand of law to apprehend the Doctor.

Progress under O'Fallon's plans, however, ceased in the face of Washington's proclamation. It cut him off from the possibility of association with the United States government and greatly weakened him in Kentucky. Wilkinson's letters to Miró had prevented any accord with the Spanish government, and it is unlikely that he ever came to the point of making arrangements with English officials.

Even his immediate employers, the South Carolina Yazoo Company, were in poor position to back him. They were facing the hopeless task of raising the required amount of specie to pay the state of Georgia for their grant. In January, 1791, they decided "to make known to the public the transactions, views and situation of the company" and to adopt a new plan for the future. The secretary prepared a history of the company and a plan for reorganization, and his report was accepted on March 3, and printed under the title, *An Extract from the Minutes of the South-Carolina Yazoo Company*. In general it was favorable to O'Fallon, although it expressed alarm at the extent of his military operations. The document says nothing about a break between O'Fallon and Wilkinson, and naturally there is no indication of the idea of separatism. It seems evident that the publication was a carefully prepared attempt at defensive propaganda.

Less than three weeks after the acceptance of the report, came President Washington's proclamation against O'Fallon. About the same time, Thomas Washington, one of the four founders of the company, was hanged for counterfeiting. In view of these facts, to say nothing of the alleged attempts of Wilkinson to discredit O'Fallon in Charleston, it was obvious that the company could not continue to support actively the work of its agent. It is worthy of note that the copy of the *Extract from the Minutes* in the possession of the Maryland Historical Society bears this manuscript inscription on the flyleaf. "To George Washington Esqr; President of the United States From His Most Ob^t. hum: Ser^t: Ax^r: Moultrie Presid^t: S^o: Car: Yaz: Com^y: July 13:th 1791." When one compares this with the letters of Moultrie and his associates in the winter of 1789–90 to Cape and Holder and Benjamin Farrar, with their strong implication of separatism, it is easy to see that the company leaders have taken to cover and their agent can expect no further support for his schemes.[79]

One more factor contributed to the collapse of the company's project. Gayoso de Lemos, the energetic Spanish Governor at Natchez, had long been alarmed at the doings of O'Fallon, and after emphatically reporting the defenselessness of Spain on the east bank of the Mississippi, had forestalled the Yazoo Company by establishing a fortified Spanish post at Nogales or Walnut Hills, below the mouth of the Yazoo and at the

point where O'Fallon planned to make his settlement.
According to Gayoso, the fortification had played no
small part in ruining the hopes of the Doctor. He reported that, after the proclamation of Washington,
O'Fallon had been obliged to live in retirement for a
time and then take to flight; and he added that since
he was a turbulent busybody, no doubt he was now
concocting some new intrigue.[80]

In May, however, O'Fallon was at the Falls of the
Ohio with the Clarks and wrote a long, newsy letter to a
brother of George Rogers Clark in Virginia. But for the
work of the Cabinet, he said, he would have been in the
Yazoo country long ago. Now he must wait until fall.
He gave the cheerful information that Clark had become temperate and implied that he himself had been
influential in this regeneration. By the bearer he sent
"a Letter . . . for M^r. Jefferson one for Genl. Moultrie,
and one for M^r. William Shurtliff, the Treasurer of the
Company," which he asked Clark to mail for him.[81]

The slow-moving Spanish Court had finally determined not to allow any American settlements between
the Tennessee and the Mississippi. In October a belated
order was issued by the Crown for the arrest of O'Fallon if he should appear at New Orleans.[82] But there was
little likelihood of his putting his head into the noose.
He had dropped his correspondence with Miró, but
he maintained that his agency for the company was still
in force. By this assumption he endeavored to keep possession of the goods salvaged from Holder and thus re-

imburse himself for losses in his unfruitful work as General Agent.[83] In reality the curtain had fallen on his project of a Yazoo colony, though hope still flickered in his breast and fear of an invasion still weighed upon the hearts of the Spaniards.

Carondelet succeeded Miró at the end of 1791 and took up the endless task of writing letters home, in which appear occasional references to the menace of Clark and O'Fallon. The latter had resumed the practice of medicine. In the fall of 1792 he was employed to care for the soldiers of the garrison at Fort Steuben,[84] and there remains a curious document which shows that he attempted to get together a group of citizens or families who would pay him by the year to keep them well.[85]

Medical practice, however, seemed rather prosaic to one who had given his life to land schemes and political adventure. Gayoso de Lemos was right. O'Fallon could not withdraw from the field of intrigue, nor cease to dream of large affairs on the international stage. He had once threatened Miró with a conquest of the Mississippi Valley and the Gulf ports under English auspices. In the latter part of the year 1792, the European situation led him to revive the enterprise but this time with a different allegiance. War between France and Spain was imminent and an attack upon Louisiana could now be planned with French backing. Before the end of the year he had concerted this new scheme with George Rogers Clark and the latter had written to the

French government proposing to recruit an army in the trans-Allegheny region which would operate under the French flag in a conquest of the Spanish posts of the Mississippi Valley. He offered his services as military commander. O'Fallon wrote at the same time to Thomas Paine, then a member of the French Convention, recommending Clark and urging his appointment.

These letters have not been found, but a letter of Paine to O'Fallon, dated February 17, 1793, tells the whole story. He acknowledged the receipt of O'Fallon's letter and stated that Clark's offer and proposals were under consideration, and his terms would, he thought, be complied with. "Mr. Jefferson's private sentiments [respecting Clark], and the reliance I have in yr. narrative, which confirms the whole, will excite every exertion on my part, to have the expedition promoted as you wish." War between France and Spain seemed to him inevitable—in fact he expected a declaration in "a week or two." The expedition, if successful, would, he thought, "promote every end" of O'Fallon's agency, since the dislodging of the Spaniards from the region of the three Georgia grants would be regarded as conquest of Spanish territory, and in that case the grants, he made no doubt, would be confirmed to the company who, by themselves or their agents, had assisted in the expedition.[83] Pointed and precious words these must have been to O'Fallon.

Independent of the suggestion of Clark and O'Fallon, the French government had been planning the

organization in the western towns of an attack upon
Louisiana, and the proposition of Clark fitted admirably into its schemes. In February the two Kentuckians, although they had not yet heard from Paine,
renewed their correspondence. On the 2d of the month,
Clark appears to have written to Genêt, outlining the
plan of the expedition and suggesting the need of about
£3,000 sterling to enable him to execute the project.[87]
Three days later another letter was written, with
Clark's name appended to it. A rough draft or copy
of it in the Draper Collection is all we have, and this
copy is in the handwriting of James O'Fallon.[88] To anyone who has read the verbose and pompous letters of
O'Fallon there will come a strong impression that not
only the handwriting but the content as well must be
credited to the Doctor rather than to the General. The
exaggerated diction, the excessive use of adjectives and
superlatives, the long-drawn-out sentence structure,
and a characteristic habit of interjecting parenthetical
phrases and clauses, all are reminiscent of O'Fallon's
style rather than that of Clark.[89]

O'Fallon apparently took this occasion to write again
to Paine, for the last paragraph of the letter of February 5 contains the statement: "Please have the inclosed
transmitted to Mr. Paine. It is from a friend of his."[90]
Genêt, on July 12, answered Clark cordially and flat-
teringly. He accepted his proposals and sent Citizen
Michaux to Kentucky as agent for the French Republic, with a provisional commission for Clark as

Commander-in-Chief of the Independent and Revolutionary Army of the Mississippi.[91]

Michaux delivered this letter and the commission in September and Clark set himself at once to the organization of his forces for the attack upon Louisiana.[92] But the invasion failed to materialize, as had the earlier projects of O'Fallon, partly through the action of President Washington and partly because of the inability of the backers to give adequate support.

Long before the dissolution of the scheme, O'Fallon had ceased to be a factor. During the year 1793 his relations with the Clark family were distinctly strained. Mrs. O'Fallon had suffered a nervous breakdown, due in part, apparently, to the determination of her husband to remove from the circle of her family and settle in Lexington.[93] Personal differences increased the estrangement and finally his wife left him, taking with her the two sons, John and Benjamin, both destined to become well-known figures in the history of the Mississippi Valley.

In 1793 O'Fallon was only forty-four years of age. His old friends had not forgotten him. In February Paine had urged him to use his literary talents in the cause of revolution: "if as yet in the habits of writing; this, My Dear Doctor, is yr. precious time. Never was there a cause so deserving of yr. pen. I have tried the force of mine, and with some success."[94] In September Anthony Wayne wrote offering him a position as senior surgeon with his expedition against the Indians.[95] But

his course was almost run. His latest known letter was
written in November, 1793.[96] It was indited in a last
spell of hope to his estranged wife and was addressed:
"My dear and lovely wife, at least, to me still lovely." His
final plea is as unconvincing as his letters to Miró. He
blames the parents and especially brother George, who,
he says, charged him with forging Anthony Wayne's
letter, with attempting to poison his son Johnny, and
with having murdered his former wife.[97] And he recounts an incident in which the General tried to strike
him but was sent sprawling to the floor by a blow from
the Doctor's fist. This is probably the same altercation
which is described—quite differently—in a letter of
Gayoso de Lemos. "O'Fallon," he wrote to Carondelet,
"has parted from his wife, who has withdrawn to the
house of Clark, her brother, and he, in resentment of
this offense has maltreated O'Fallon, even going so far
as to break his stick over his head, inflicting injuries
from which he had not yet recovered at Mitchel's departure."[98]

We do not know the exact date or manner of O'Fallon's death. Tradition has it that he was thrown from
a horse while making a trip east and that he died from
the injuries which he received.[99] The records of the
courthouse in Louisiana, Kentucky, reveal nothing;
but an old ledger discloses the fact that in March, 1794,
William Croghan paid fees as administrator of the estate of James O'Fallon,[100] and another contemporary
manuscript shows that on May 6 the goods of the de-

parted Doctor were sold at public auction.[101] His effects seem pitifully few for one who boasted in 1788 that his professional income was far in excess of the 1,500 guineas per year which he asked from Spain.

O'Fallon's feverish and erratic life was over. He had spent his years fishing in troubled waters and to little avail. Yet he was not without ability. Even Wilkinson described him as a man of erudtion and much talent, though lacking in the judgment necessary for great enterprises.[102] Possessed of personality, and convincing in his first impressions, he was inherently wanting in character, and he fell short in the quality of leadership required. He could stir the interest of men like Wilkinson and Sevier and Clark, but he could not command the situation and maintain their allegiance. As an intriguer he had great handicaps. He was bold but not farsighted, ready with attack but utterly lacking in finesse, full of mendacity but surpassingly maladroit in his operations. And he played his game in the West against a man as unscrupulous as himself and far more astute and clever.

The ill-starred fortunes of O'Fallon were, nevertheless, of greater significance than their lack of success would indicate. His schemes were by no means mere local projects. In scope they embraced the whole of the Valley and affected a variety of nations. Beyond question the situation in the West from 1790 to 1793 afforded an unusual opportunity for a master manipulator, and O'Fallon's backing was strong and his initial contacts with frontier leaders widespread and effective. His first plan—an independent enterprise with Spanish alliance,—if it had been handled more wisely and had been supported by Wilkinson, might have succeeded, and perhaps might have led to a separation of the entire trans-Allegheny region. The second phase—the establishment of his colony by force of arms in spite of Spanish resistance—was so important as to alarm and bring action from the governments of two nations; while the scheme which O'Fallon and Clark fomented in 1792 for an attack upon Louisiana on behalf of France involved one more nation in the group which watched with intense interest the movements of those who lived upon the "western waters."

The wisdom of Washington, the wiles of Wilkinson, the menace of the Indians, were factors in his defeat. Perhaps more fundamentally, his consistent failure may be attributed to his own blundering incapacity and to the western individualism which through all these years wrecked the very schemes of separatism which it fostered. But the persistent audacity of O'Fallon and the recklessness with which he played his swashbuckling role in the West made his intrigues a continuing threat to both Spain and the United States, and presented possible opportunities for both England and France. His machinations form, therefore, not only an important chapter in the history of separatism, but also an essential as well as a colorful part of the larger story of the international struggle for the Mississippi Valley.

NOTES

[1] Draper MSS, 34 J 20–23, Library of the State Historical Society of Wisconsin. To the document is added the following statement by the son, John O'Fallon: "The foregoing is taken from the Pedigree or narrative of my father Dr James O'Fallon which I recd when about 21 years of age, from Major Croghan. . . ." See also, *ibid.*, 34 J 12, 18, for information contributed by John O'Fallon, and *ibid.*, 4 CC 171, for a brief account of the Irish ancestors of James O'Fallon. Cf. Burke, *A Genealogical and Heraldic Dictionary of the Landed Gentry in Great Britain and Ireland* (1855), p. 366.

[2] The names of graduates, by years, are given in *List of the Graduates in Medicine in the University of Edinburgh, from MDCCV to MDCCCLXVI* (Edinburgh, 1867). The name of James Fallon, or of James O'Fallon, does not appear in the list. He was perhaps granted a license to practice medicine by the Royal College of Physicians and Surgeons of Edinburgh, or some other institution of that type.

[3] Draper MSS, 34 J 20.

[4] *Ibid.*, 34 J 21.

[5] *Ibid.*

[6] *North Carolina Colonial Records*, X, 410. Beginning with Vol. XI, these are known as *North Carolina State Records*. Cited hereafter as *N.C.C.R.* and *N.C.S.R.*, respectively.

[7] *Ibid.*, p. 418.

[8] *Ibid.*, pp. 412, 419–420.

[9] *Ibid.*, p. 422.

[10] Draper MSS, 34 J 20–23.

[11] *Pennsylvania Archives* (3d ser.), XXIII, 396. The name "Fallon, James, Surgeon" appears under "Hospital Department" in a list entitled "Miscellaneous Rolls—Soldiers of Pennsylvania Line—1777–1780."

[12] Fallon to Burke, April 1, 1779, *N.C.S.R.*, XIV, 49–50.

[13] The names of James Fallon and "Doct'r Fallon" appear on a tax list for the city of Philadelphia for the year 1782. *Pa. Arch.* (3d ser.), XVI, 325, 333. The identification of these references with the subject of this sketch is of course only conjectural.

[14] Gaillard Hunt (ed.), *Journals of the Continental Congress, 1774–1789* (Washington, 1914), XXII, 4.

[15] Joseph Meredith Toner, "Medical Men of the American Revolution," Vol. V, Division of Manuscripts, Library of Congress. See *Penn-*

sylvania Colonial Records, XIII, 170, and XIV, 192, for action by the
Council of Pennsylvania on the recommendation of Congress.

¹⁶ Draper MSS, 34 J 22. In the Toner MSS is a statement that Fallon
sailed "on board the South Carolina Oct. 1782 from Philadelphia &
off the capes of the Delaware, surrendered to 2 British Frigates." Toner
does not give the source of his information and the facts are rather
against its acceptance. See Gardner W. Allen, *A Naval History of the
American Revolution* (Boston, 1913), II, 583–586, and Charles O.
Paullin, *The Navy of the American Revolution* (Cleveland, 1906), pp.
438–439, for the story of the *South Carolina* and its commander, Alexander Gillon. See also a biographical sketch of Gillon in *South Carolina Historical and Genealogical Magazine,* I, 32–33.

¹⁷ Archibald Maclaine to George Hooper, March 25, 1783, *N.C.S.R.*,
XVI, 951.

¹⁸ The story of this radical democratic movement under the leadership of Gillon and Fallon is well told by Ulrich B. Phillips in "The
South Carolina Federalists," *American Historical Review,* XIV, 533–
537.

¹⁹ *Gazette of the State of South Carolina,* November 27, 1783. See
also issues for April and May, 1784.

²⁰ Issue for May 13, 1784.

²¹ See also Phillips, "S.C. Federalists," *Am. Hist Rev.,* XIV, 534, for
reference to an earlier attack upon Fallon in the *Georgia Gazette.*

²² Archibald Maclaine to George Hooper, December 23, 1783, September 28, 1784, *N.C.S.R.*, XVI, 997, XVII, 169. Other references to
Fallon are in letters dated August 23 and December 16, 1783; January
17 and June 25, 1784, *ibid.,* XVI, 977, 992, XVII, 125, 151. In the
printed reproduction of these letters the name appears in three forms:
Fallon, Tallon, and Tullon. But the facts stated in the letters of December 23, 1783, and January 17, 1784, prove that the references are to
the same man.

²³ Phillips, "S. C. Federalists," *Am. Hist. Rev.,* XIV, 537.

²⁴ The identity of James Fallon and James O'Fallon is proved by
the fact that O'Fallon in his sketch of his life which was handed down
to his son recounts, though with some distortion, the events which
are portrayed by other sources for the life of James Fallon.

²⁵ O'Fallon to Gardoqui, May 26, 1788, Gardoqui Papers, I, 198–260,
Durrett Collection, University of Chicago Library. This is a manuscript copy of a Spanish translation and covers, in the case of the letter,
12 pages, and in the case of the document, 51 pages, a typical instance
of O'Fallon's extreme wordiness.

²⁶ Gardoqui to Floridablanca, July 25, 1788, Gardoqui Papers, I, 196–197.

²⁷ O'Fallon to Miró, May 24, 1790. Charles Gayarré, *History of Louisiana* (New Orleans, 1903), III, 291–292.

²⁸ Arthur P. Whitaker, *The Spanish-American Frontier: 1783–1795* (Boston, 1927), 128.

²⁹ Wilkinson to Gardoqui, January 1, 1789; Wilkinson to Miró, February 12 and 14, 1789. These letters are printed in Gayarré, *op. cit.*, III, 247–251, 223–247. See particularly pp. 234, 242–243, 251. Cf. Whitaker, *op. cit.*, p. 129.

³⁰ Charles H. Haskins, "The Yazoo Land Companies," American Historical Association, *Papers*, V, Part 4, p. 65; Whitaker, *op. cit.*, p. 129.

³¹ Letter of James O'Fallon to the editor, Mr. Bradford, in the *Kentucky Gazette*, March 31, 1792. This lengthy epistle, continued in the issue of April 7, contains much information about the organization and activities of the company. See, also, *An Extract from the Minutes of the South-Carolina Yazoo Company* (Charleston, 1791), I, 17–18, 36–37, 40–41. This printed book, prepared by the secretary of the company, consists of three parts and numerous appendixes. Part I is a history of the company and an invaluable source, although as Professor Haskins points out, the volume reveals merely those facts and purposes which the company wished the public to know. The present writer has had access to the material through a photostatic reproduction of a copy in the possession of the Maryland Historical Society. The promotion activities of the company are clearly shown in two letters written by Alexander Moultrie in January and February, 1790. One is to Benjamin Farrar, a wealthy planter in the Natchez district and a Spanish subject. The other is to Alexander McGillivray, the famous Creek chieftain. These documents are printed with editorial notes by Dr. Arthur P. Whitaker, under the heading "The South Carolina Yazoo Company," in the *Mississippi Valley Historical Review*, XVI, 383–394.

³² Thomas Washington to John Cape, September 20, 1789; Moultrie, Snipes, and Huger to Holder, October 1, 1789. These letters are found in the Spanish translation in the transcripts in the Department of Archives and History (Jackson, Miss.), Mississippi Provincial Archives, Spanish Dominion, III, 441–448. They are printed in Manuel Serrano y Sanz, *Documentos Históricos de la Florida y la Luisiana*, pp. 383–387. A number of documents relating to James O'Fallon were examined by the present writer in the Spanish archives several years ago. In the present study, however, the Spanish archival material has been

consulted largely in transcript form in the Library of Congress, the Newberry Library in Chicago, the Durrett Collection, the Mississippi Department of Archives and History, and the Louisiana Historical Society in New Orleans. Therefore the citations to sources will be to these transcripts.

³³ Wilkinson to Miró, January 26, 1790, Archivo General de Indias (cited hereafter as A.G.I.), Audiencia de Santo Domingo, 86-6-18 (Miss. Prov. Arch., III, 439–441). This letter is printed in Serrano y Sanz, *op. cit.,* pp. 382–383. Gayarré, *op. cit.,* III, 276–277, also quotes extracts from this letter, retranslated into English, but he wrongly dates the letter January 20. The transcripts which he used, now in the Louisiana Historical Society library, give the date January 26 with an alternative date 20 above the 26.

³⁴ Wilkinson to Moultrie, Huger, Snipes, and Washington, January 4, 1790, enclosed with the letters cited in the preceding note, in Miró's No. 49 *reservada* to Valdez, Miss. Prov. Arch., III, 448–455; printed in Serrano y Sanz, *op. cit.,* pp. 387–390. This letter states also that Wilkinson had received, in the preceding April, a letter from Thomas Washington, dated February 21, 1789, discussing the Georgia land project. In the *Minutes S. C. Yazoo Co.,* I, 24, is an abstract of Wilkinson's letter to the company. In this version Wilkinson is quoted as recommending the appointment of a proper person (presumably himself) to negotiate with Spanish officials, suggesting Innes, Muter, Nicholas, and Sebastian as leading Kentuckians whose services the company should secure, and offering to act in coöperation with an agent whom the company should send out to Kentucky. The reply of the company is represented as an offer to admit Wilkinson to a large share in the purchase and to admit his four friends "to one-twentieth each, on equal terms with the other proprietors" (p. 25).

³⁵ Aside from the four original members of the company (Washington, Huger, Snipes, and Alexander Moultrie), the sketch of O'Fallon in the Draper MSS names six others of the twenty making up the enlarged group. These are: O'Fallon, Gen. William Moultrie, recently Governor of South Carolina, and "Gov Telfair, Judges Osborne and Walton and Col McIntosh of Georgia." Draper MSS, 34 J 20–23.

³⁶ That O'Fallon came to Kentucky equipped with a commission, general instructions, and secret instructions is attested by O'Fallon himself (*Kentucky Gazette,* April 7, 1792) and by the secretary of the S. C. Yazoo Company (*Minutes S. C. Yazoo Co.,* I, 26–28). The text of general instructions described above is in the Draper MSS, V 73. Their identification as the general rather than the secret instructions is

founded on their precise correspondence with the provisions of the general instructions as specifically paraphrased by the secretary from the records of the company. *Minutes S. C. Yazoo Co.*, I, 26–28.

[37] O'Fallon to John Sevier, April 7, 1790, Draper MSS, 5 XX 23. See also Alexander Moultrie to John Sevier, March 8, 1790, *ibid.*, V 72. This was written in answer to one from Sevier to Moultrie, February 11, 1790. Cf. O'Fallon to Bryan Bruin, May 13, 1790, and O'Fallon to Col. Bryan Bruin (son of preceding), in Louisiana Manuscripts, Bancroft Library, Berkeley, Calif.

[38] Alexander Moultrie to James Wilkinson, February 27, 1790 (Miss. Prov. Arch., III, 473–476). Cf. note 34 above.

[39] Gayarré, *op. cit.*, III, 293. See also letter, Miró to Las Casas, October 7, 1790, No. 9, *res.*, discussing the relations of Wilkinson and O'Fallon, A.G.I., Papeles de Cuba, legajo 1446, photographic copies of dispatches to the captains general of Cuba, Division of Manuscripts, Library of Congress.

[40] Miró to Wilkinson, April 30, 1790, Gayarré, *op. cit.*, III, 281–282.

[41] O'Fallon to Miró, May 24, 1790, *ibid.*, pp. 288–293. The letter is here retranslated into English and printed in full except for one brief sentence.

[42] O'Fallon to Miró, July 16, 1790. The original of this letter was retained by Miró and later sent to Wilkinson to be used against O'Fallon. It is probably no longer in existence. A copy was sent by Miró to Las Casas, Captain General at Havana, in Miró's letter of October 7, 1790, No. 9, *res.* Another copy was sent to Wilkinson for the purpose of eliciting more information on the situation in Kentucky. When, some time later, the original also was sent to Wilkinson, a copy in English was made. This copy is among the Louisiana Manuscripts, Bancroft Library. It covers twelve pages written in a fine hand.

[43] Miró to Valdez, August 10, 1790, A.G.I., Aud. de Santo Dom., 86-6-18 (Miss, Prov. Arch., III, 457–473). Gayarré (*op. cit.*, III, 293–300) gives an extended résumé of Miró's report.

[44] Miró to Wilkinson, September 20, 1790, A.G.I., Pap. de Cuba, leg. 2362 (Newberry Lib. transcripts).

[45] Miró to Las Casas, October 7, 1790, No. 9, *res.*, A.G.I., Pap. de Cuba, leg. 1446 (Lib. of Cong. trans.).

[46] Miró to O'Fallon, September 30, 1790, A.G.I., Papeles de Estado, leg. 9 (these are Newberry Lib. trans.). O'Fallon does not, in any of his six communications to Miró prior to March, 1791, mention receiving an answer from the Spanish Governor; and Miró, in a letter of May 8, 1791, to Las Casas, quotes Wilkinson to the effect that the

messenger had informed him that he had not delivered the note to O'Fallon. *Ibid.*

[47] *American State Papers, Indian Affairs*, I, 115–117.

[48] *Minutes S. C. Yazoo Co.*, I, 31–34.

[49] Moultrie to Wilkinson, September 5, 1790, A.G.I., Pap. de Est., leg. 9.

[50] Wilkinson to Moultrie, October 20, 1790. The gist of this letter is given by Wilkinson in a letter to Miró, March 17, 1791, and it is referred to by date in a letter, Wilkinson to Moultrie, November 4, 1790, *ibid.* A portion of the letter is quoted in *Minutes S. C. Yazoo Co.*, I, 35–36.

[51] *Ibid.*, pp. 34–35.

[52] *Ibid.*, p. 37.

[53] *Ibid.*, pp. 38–39. The letter is here given in extenso, if it is not a complete transcript. O'Fallon reported that Nolan, who lay very ill of a fever, had sent a confidential messenger urging strongly that the time was ripe for action, while Spaniards and Indians were favorable. O'Fallon therefore had "closed with the golden moment of opportunity, and resolved instantly to send down as many of our troops . . . as would consent to go." Philip Nolan had long been an agent of Wilkinson's. He had been the messenger who conveyed O'Fallon's letter of May 24 to Miró. It is probable that Wilkinson lent his agent to O'Fallon with wisdom aforethought.

[54] This item as printed in the *Kentucky Gazette*, February 26, 1791, covers three columns of type.

[55] See also letter of O'Fallon to General Charles Scott, September 4, 1790, urging the latter's participation in the project. Division of Manuscripts, Library of Congress.

[56] Wilkinson to Miró, December 16, 1790, A.G.I., Pap. de Est., leg. 9.

[57] Wilkinson to Miró, March 17, 1791. This letter and its enclosures— O'Fallon to Wilkinson (without date), Moultrie to Wilkinson, September 5, 1790, and Wilkinson to Moultrie, November 4, 1790,—translated into Spanish, are found enclosed in a letter, Miró to Las Casas, May 8, 1791, *ibid.* The undated O'Fallon letter, dealing briefly with a rumor of Spanish incitement of the Indians against the projected colony, was characterized by Wilkinson in his correspondence with Miró as an "Extraordinary note" and was made the explanation of his break with the Doctor. Since the only record we have of the letter of O'Fallon to Wilkinson and of Wilkinson to Moultrie of November 4, 1790, is in the form of copies transmitted by Wilkinson, it is possible that these were either fabricated or distorted by him to serve

his purposes in March, 1791. This theory has some support in the fact that he did not mention the O'Fallon note in his letter to Miró in December, and in the fact that the secretary of the S. C. Yazoo Company in the *Minutes S. C. Yazoo Co.*, makes no reference to any letter from Wilkinson to the company severing his connection. The report of the secretary was finished and presented to the company on March 3, 1791.

[58] Wilkinson to Miró, March 17, 1791, A.G.I., Pap. de Est., leg. 9. Wilkinson's claim that he had reduced O'Fallon's battalion to 50 men is rather vitiated by a letter written by Wilkinson himself on February 14, 1791, to Philip Nolan: "O'Fallon is here [in Frankfort] making wonderful exertions: has engaged General Clark to command his troops, and has made extensive contracts for provisions, negroes, horses, etc. The company offered me 20,000 acres as a compliment, but I finally rejected it." J. F. H. Claiborne, *Mississippi as a Province, Territory, and State* (Jackson, 1880), I, 157 n.

[59] The text of this proclamation has not been found, so far as the writer can ascertain, but the contents are clearly stated by Washington himself, who referred to it in his later proclamation of March 19, 1791 (see text in the *Kentucky Gazette,* May 14, 1791), and by Secretary of War Knox in a report dated January 22, 1791 (*Am. St. Paps., Ind. Affs.*, I, 112), and again in his instructions to General St. Clair, March 21, 1791, *ibid.*, 172.

[60] Unfortunately, the original of O'Fallon's letter is not available. Although Dr. J. F. Jameson kindly instituted a search in the collections of the Library of Congress as well as in the files of the Secretary of the Senate, the document could not be found. William Maclay, who heard it read in the Senate, January 24, 1791, comments upon it in his *Journal* (New York, 1927). The Secretary of the S. C. Yazoo Company describes it briefly in the *Minutes S. C. Yazoo Co.*, I, 32–33, giving a dispatch of O'Fallon's as the basis of his information and stating that the letter was written on the advice of General St. Clair. The most detailed account of the document is in a letter from John Brown to James Wilkinson, February 10, 1791, a copy of which the latter sent to Miró enclosed in his own letter of March 19, 1791, A.G.I., Pap. de Est., leg. 9. Neither Maclay nor the secretary of the company mentions any revelations as to Kentucky separatists, and in the absence of the original document the question may well be raised, whether Wilkinson in reporting Brown's letter to Miró did not add the item about these disclosures for the sake of putting himself in a strategic position with the Spanish officials.

Both Maclay and Brown refer to the O'Fallon letter as of the date September 30. In the *Am. St. Paps., Ind. Affs.*, I, 115, is a short letter from O'Fallon to Washington dated September 25, and written, as O'Fallon said, "since the sealing up of the despatches herein enclosed to your Excellency." It would seem, therefore, that either the dates were confused or O'Fallon wrote twice to Washington.

[61] John Williams to Gayoso de Lemos, January 16, 1791, A.G.I., Pap. de Est., leg. 9.

[62] As to the truth of the statement that McGillivray was a fellow proprietor, there is some doubt. The Secretary of the company states that he was. *Minutes S. C. Yazoo Co.*, I, 20. But see Whitaker, "Alexander McGillivray, 1789–1793," *North Carolina Historical Review*, V, 295–296.

[63] O'Fallon to Miró, December 17, 1790, A.G.I., Pap. de Est., leg. 9.

[64] O'Fallon to Miró, January 15, 1791, *ibid.*

[65] O'Fallon to Miró, February 18, 1791, *ibid.*

[66] Miró to O'Fallon, March 26, 1791, *ibid.*

[67] O'Fallon to Jonathan Clark, May 30, 1791, Draper MSS, 2 L 28.

[68] This document is preserved in the manuscript collection of the Missouri Historical Society, St. Louis.

[69] *Ibid.*

[70] Maclay, *op. cit.*, p. 367.

[71] *Journal of the Senate of the United States,* January 24, 1791.

[72] John Brown to Wilkinson, February 10, 1791. The only form in which the writer has found this letter is in a Spanish translation of a *copia literal* received from Wilkinson by Miró in a letter of March 19, 1791. The Spanish translation is one of the enclosures in Miró's letter to Las Casas, May 8, 1791, No. 25, *res.*, Pap. de Est., leg. 9. With respect to the authenticity of the letter see note 60 above.

[73] Wilkinson to Miró, March 19, 1791, A.G.I., Pap. de Est., leg. 9.

[74] Miro to Las Casas, May 8, 1791, No. 25, *res., ibid.* Apparently Miró later decided to send the original to Wilkinson, for the English copy of O'Fallon's letter of July 16, 1790 (in the Bancroft Library), bears this annotation, *"Es copia de la original corregida que se remitio al Gen¹ Wilkinson en carta de Dⁿ Estevan Miró de 25 de Enº de 1792. Andres Armesto."*

[75] This proclamation was printed in the *Kentucky Gazette,* May 14, 1791.

[76] See letter of Thomas Jefferson, Secretary of State, to George Nicholas, Attorney of the District of Kentucky, March 22, 1791, directing him to "proceed against the said O'Fallon according to law," Paul

Leicester Ford (ed.), *Writings of Thomas Jefferson* (New York, 1895), V, 305–306; also "Instructions to Major General Arthur St. Clair" by Henry Knox, March 21, 1791, *Am. St. Paps., Ind. Affs.*, I, 172.

[77] Draper MSS, 54 J 20.

[78] Wilkinson to Miró, March 31, 1791, A.G.I., Pap. de Cuba, leg. 2374. In reading a paper on O'Fallon at the meeting of the Mississippi Valley Historical Association in 1928, I stated that, although I had no proof of it, I was convinced that the anonymous letter had been written by Wilkinson for the purpose of driving O'Fallon out of the country. Professor Arthur P. Whitaker, who heard the paper, remarked that he had seen a letter from Wilkinson admitting the authorship of such a communication, and later he kindly sent me the quotation and citation used above. He added the statement: "A letter that is apparently the copy just mentioned is in *ibid*. It is endorsed at the end, 'Copy of an Anonymous Letter to Dr. O'Fallon: J. Wilkinson', and is dated March 31, 1794 (i.e. 1791)."

[79] For indication of Washington's attitude toward the Yazoo companies, see J. C. Fitzpatrick (ed.), *Diaries of George Washington* (Boston, 1925), IV, 157, 192, 196.

[80] Gayoso de Lemos to Floridablanca, January 7, 1792, A.G.I., Pap. de Cuba, leg. 177 (Newberry Lib. trans.) . Gayoso wrote two long letters on this date to Floridablanca. With respect to the fortifications at Walnut Hills, see also Hastings, "Yazoo Land Companies," Am. Hist. Assoc., *Papers*, V, Part 4, p. 73 n.

[81] O'Fallon to Jonathan Clark, May 30, 1791, Draper MSS, 2 L 28.

[82] Floridablanca to Miró, October, 1791, A.G.I., Pap. de Cuba, leg. 177 (Newberry Lib. trans.).

[83] *Kentucky Gazette,* April 7, 1792.

[84] Draper MSS, 4 CC 174.

[85] *Ibid.,* p. 168.

[86] This letter from Paine to O'Fallon was published with an introduction by Dr. Louise P. Kellogg in the *Am. Hist. Rev.*, XXIX, 501–505.

[87] The contents of this letter are known to us through a document in the French archives headed *Extrait de la lettre écritte par le Général Clarke au Citoyen Genêt.* . . . In reality it is an abstract of the letter made by Genêt, rather than an extract. It is published by Professor Turner in his "Correspondence of Clark and Genêt," Am. Hist. Assoc., *Annual Report*, 1896, I, 971–972.

[88] This letter is printed *ibid.,* pp. 967–971. See Professor Turner's note, *ibid.,* p. 967. The letter is from the Draper MSS and is without address. It is perhaps the same one that John O'Fallon, in a letter to

Lyman Draper in 1847, refers to as being from Clark to President Washington, dated in February, 1793, and in the handwriting of James O'Fallon. *Ibid.*, 34 J 12.

[89] This theory has some corroboration in a letter from O'Fallon to Captain Herron dated October 18, 1793, and quoted in M. D. Conway, *The Life of Thomas Paine* (New York, 1892), II, 156, as follows: "This plan [an attack on Louisiana] was digested between Gen. Clarke and me last Christmas. I framed the whole of the correspondence in the General's name, and corroborated it by a private letter of my own to Mr. Thomas Paine, of the National Assembly, with whom during the late war I was very intimate." See note by Professor Turner in Am. Hist. Assoc., *Ann. Rept.*, 1903, II, 199. Further support is given to the general theory of O'Fallon's function as a letter writer for the General in a statement by Gayoso de Lemos, the Spanish Governor at Natchez: "As soon as Clark accepted the proposals the French commissioners made him, he asked O'Fallon to write a French letter for him to the Minister Genêt; he did so and was much applauded. . . ." Gayoso to Carondelet, December 23, 1793, *ibid.*, 1896, I, 1031.

[90] Ternant, predecessor of Genêt as representative of France in the United States, wrote as follows in a letter of May 10, 1793, to the Minister of Foreign Affairs: *"Je joins encore à la présente, une lettre que je viens de recevoir de Kentucky pour Thomas Payne de la convention—Cette lettre étoit accompagnée d'une proposition intéressante du Général Clark sur la Louisianne, que je mettrai sous les yeux de mon Successeur dès son arrivée ici."* *Ibid.*, 1903, II, 199.

[91] *Ibid.*, 1896, I, 986.

[92] *Ibid.*, pp. 1007–1009.

[93] John Clark to O'Fallon, May 28, 1792, Draper MSS, 4 CC 172; O'Fallon to John Clark, July 15 and 16, 1793, Draper MSS, 2 M 45, 46; O'Fallon to Mrs. O'Fallon, November 23, 1793, Draper MSS, 2 M 47. Mrs. O'Fallon lived for a time at least with her husband in Lexington, since the younger son Benjamin was born there. J. T. Scharf, *History of St. Louis City and County* (Philadelphia, 1883), I, 344.

[94] Thomas Paine to O'Fallon, February 17, 1793, *Am. Hist. Rev.*, XXIX, 505.

[95] Anthony Wayne to O'Fallon, September 16, 1793, Am. Hist. Assoc., *Ann. Rept.*, 1896, I, 1000–1001.

[96] O'Fallon to Mrs. O'Fallon, November 23, 1793, Draper MSS, 2 M 47.

[97] This is the only reference the writer has found to any former marriage of O'Fallon.

[98] Gayoso to Carondelet, December 23, 1793 (extract), Am. Hist. Assoc., *Ann. Rept.*, 1896, I, 1031.

[99] For this information I am indebted to Mr. R. C. Ballard Thruston of the Filson Club. Mr. Thruston and Mr. Otto Rothert kindly examined the courthouse records in Louisville in an effort to find evidence of the death of O'Fallon.

[100] Ledger to William Croghan, p. 94, Durrett Collection.

[101] "Account of Sales of Sundry Articles belonging to the Estate of Doctor James O'Fallon." MS in Missouri Historical Society collection.

[102] Wilkinson to Miró, February 14, 1791, A.G.I., Pap. de Est., leg. 9.

JOHN STUART
AND THE CARTOGRAPHY OF
THE INDIAN BOUNDARY LINE

·◄ ❉ ▸·

THE MOVING borderland that marked the advance of English and Americans westward from the Atlantic was not a single line. Always there were two lines closely paralleling each other: one, the advancing edge of the white man's settlements; the other, the retreating line of the Indian tribes. Hence it was logical that there should arise the idea of an Indian boundary line forming a third parallel within the intervening zone. But not until the crisis of 1763 was a general line laid down. In point of fact, that year saw the inauguration of two widely different types of boundary. One was a general emergency line, established by fiat of the King in the Proclamation of 1763 and determined as at the heads of the streams flowing into the Atlantic. The other was the first section of what came to be known as the Indian boundary line. Perhaps it would be better described as the Indian treaty line, for it was a matter of agreement between whites and reds gathered in formal conferences. The boundary was specified with great care and detail and was intended to be surveyed and marked for the benefit of all parties.

This first fragment of the Indian treaty line was laid down at the Congress at Augusta, Georgia, in November, 1763, in which John Stuart, Superintendent of Indian Affairs for the Southern Department, and the four provincial governors within his territory met the Indians of all the southern tribes. A specific boundary line was drawn between the Creek Indians and Georgia, a reservation was laid out for the Catawbas, and informal understandings were entered into as to boundaries with the Creeks and Choctaws along the Gulf and with the Cherokees north of Georgia.

This was the beginning. Throughout the rest of Stuart's career as Superintendent of Indian Affairs for the Southern Department (he held the office for seventeen years, from 1762 to 1779) there was practically no time in which he was not engaged in making or revising, surveying or marking, the boundary line, and trying to keep peace between the encroaching whites and the resentful reds. Although he did not possess the high political talents of his colleague in the north, Sir William Johnson, his services to the Empire in connection with boundary disputes and cartography were longer and more important than those of the baronet.

It is not the intention of this paper, however, to trace Stuart's delineation of the boundary, but to make some observations on the contemporary maps of the line. I shall disregard printed maps and limit myself to the consideration of manuscript maps, of which there are certainly twenty (and probably many more) showing a part or all of the boundary line. A large number of these maps emanated directly or indirectly from John Stuart, many of them present information not to be gained elsewhere, and several of them solve problems which have been baffling to students of printed documents and original written sources. Most of the maps are in official repositories in London, and some are in the libraries of this country.

The first map to invite attention has to do with the Proclamation of 1763. It is one which the Board of Trade annexed to its report of June 8, 1763, looking forward to the famous Proclamation of October 7. The text of the report merely urges that a line be fixed, but it adds this remark: "In order, however, that your Majesty may judge with the greater precision of the limits of Canada as above described and also of those we shall propose for Florida, and of the Country we think right to be left as Indian Territory, we humbly beg leave to refer to the annexed chart in which those limits are particularly delineated."

Professor Alvord in his "Genesis of the Proclamation of 1763" rightly said that this map, if it could be found, would immediately settle the question as to the ideas of the Board of Trade prior to receiving the news of Pontiac's War, but he stated that search had been made for it without success. And in his later work on *The Mississippi Valley in British Politics* he still reported it as lost. Analyzing other sources, however, particularly the writings of John Pownall, he came to the conclusion

that the intended line of that date ran west of the mountains in the rear of Virginia, because of settlements in
the Upper Ohio Valley, but that to the north and south
it fell short of the divide because of claims of the Iroquois and the southern Indians to lands east of the
mountains.

But the "annexed chart" was not lost. It had become
detached from the report in the Public Record Office
in London, but was later found and inserted in the volume with a note by an official of the Record Office that
this was presumably the "annexed chart" mentioned
on page 26 of the report. The identification seems not
open to question. It is a map by Emanuel Bowen, bearing upon it, marked by hand, the outlines of the proposed colonies of Canada and the Floridas and the
location of the line setting off the Indian territory.[1]
True to the hypothesis of Professor Alvord, it shows a
western salient beyond the mountains, including the
land back of Virginia as far as the juncture of the Ohio
and the Kanawha. But instead of making the concessions to the Indians north and south of this salient, the
delineation follows with considerable fidelity the heads
of the streams flowing into the Atlantic, as finally announced in the Proclamation.

A few weeks after the report of June 8, news of Pontiac's War reached England, and in the final Proclamation of October 7 the Virginia salient was wiped out
and the more "conspicuous landmark" (as Alvord ex-

---

[1] For notes see pages 145–146.

presses it) of the headwaters of the Atlantic streams was substituted.

Thereafter, the history of the Indian boundary or treaty line under Great Britain falls into three periods: the years of tentative arrangements, 1763–1768, the year 1768, in which formal consolidation and ratification were secured, and the decade following, in which the line was subject to constant pressure and change.

Johnson in the year 1765 talked over with the Iroquois a line running from the upper Susquehanna southwestwardly to the Ohio, down that river to the Tennessee, and up the Tennessee to its source. In the same year Stuart treated with the Choctaws at Mobile and the Creeks at Pensacola, for a line roughly paralleling the Gulf Coast and thus limiting West Florida settlements. At Picolata, near St. Augustine, later in the year, he arranged with the Creeks for a boundary back of East Florida. With slight revision the Augusta line of 1763 served for Georgia, and with the Cherokees in the next two years Stuart established a line back of the Carolinas and Virginia reaching the Ohio at the mouth of the Kanawha.

The Board of Trade then collated the information sent in by the Superintendents and issued a report advising a consolidation of the line, marking their recommendations on a map.[2] Johnson and Stuart were to bring their lines together at the mouth of the Kanawha, thus restoring the westward salient proposed before the Proclamation of 1763. Johnson was specifically warned against running his line down the Ohio to the Tennessee and thus including Kentucky in the Iroquois cession, lest this make trouble with the Cherokees. Instructions in conformity with these recommendations were issued, and in the latter part of 1768 Johnson met the Iroquois at Fort Stanwix, and Stuart treated with the Cherokees and Creeks at Hard Labor and Augusta. There was tacit acceptance of the line behind West Florida.

Apparently a definitive line had now been established. It ran a far different course from the Proclamation line of 1763. Back of Virginia and Pennsylvania a salient containing many thousands of square miles stretched beyond the mountains to the Ohio River. North of this wedge of advance the line ran many miles east of the heads of Atlantic streams, and in the south it likewise receded toward the coast. But even this line was not destined to be definitive. It was modified five times in the next decade, and manuscript maps throw light on each modification.

There are at least half a dozen maps which illustrate this line of 1768. The most interesting of these is a dim, disfigured chart drawn by or for two semiofficial but very much interested observers, Dr. Thomas Walker and General Andrew Lewis. The map is valuable not only because of its graphic portrayal of that portion of the line of 1768 in which they were highly interested, but also because of its relation to later changes. It tells the story, in large part, of the break which was made

almost immediately in the line back of Virginia. Walker
and Lewis had been named by Virginia to attend the
boundary congresses as commissioners and protect and
advance the interests of their colony. They went first
to Fort Stanwix, where proceedings were so delayed
that Walker alone remained, while Lewis apparently
hurried south to attend Stuart's conference.

At Fort Stanwix, Sir William Johnson, much to
Walker's satisfaction, was persuaded by the Six Nations to exceed the instructions limiting him to the
Kanawha and allow the Iroquois to bestow upon the
King the country of Kentucky, where they disputed
claims with the Cherokees. To Virginia this grant
would pave the way for an almost unlimited advance
of speculators. Lewis, however, was too late for Stuart's
congress at Hard Labor, and his disappointment is expressed by his brother in a letter to William Preston in
January, 1769: "Some days ago I received a letter from
Andw at Williamsburgh from that place he is gone to
Charlestown and expects to go from thence to yᵉ Borders of yᵉ Cherokee Country in order to adjust something relating to treating with yᵉ Indians—it being
suposed yᵗ both intendent [i.e., Stuart] and Indians
are on a wrong Sent, at least one very different from
what we intend."⁸ The difficulty, of course, was that Sir
William Johnson, breaking with his instructions to
meet Stuart's line at the mouth of the Kanawha, had
opened Kentucky to the Virginians by grant from the
Iroquois, only to find his action negatived by the treaty

made by Stuart by which the Cherokees still retained
the control of the country as far east as the valley of
the Kanawha.

Walker and Lewis at once made a report to Governor
Botetourt of Virginia, accompanying their statement
with their map, which is full of interesting detail. It
shows the line extending down the Ohio to the mouth
of the Tennessee River, thus including Kentucky. It
quite neglects Stuart's Hard Labor line, but lays out a
tract taking in the eastern part of Kentucky and bearing the legend, "The land included within these [red]
pricked lines to be purchased of the Cherokees."[4]

Such was to be the new policy of Virginia—namely, a
fresh treaty with the Cherokees which would open up
the eastern part of Kentucky. The map foreshadows a
still greater demand. A dotted line, a continuation of
the southern boundary of Virginia, cuts westward to
the mouth of the Ohio. The land thus indicated and
comprising practically the present state of Kentucky
was asked for a few months later by the House of Bur-
gesses. A treaty to this effect with the Cherokees would
match that made by Johnson with the Iroquois.

In pursuit of this policy, the Virginians, led by
Walker and Lewis, Botetourt, and the House of Bur-
gesses, brought such pressure to bear that instructions
were issued to Stuart for a new congress. Stuart in-
sisted, however, on protecting the Cherokees in their
hunting grounds in Kentucky and urged merely an ex-
tension large enough to cover the actual Virginia set-

tlements. Governor Botetourt acceded to this, and at
Lochaber in October, 1770, a new congress was held
which added a large triangle extending west as far as
the Holston River near the Long Island.[5]

So the matter seemed settled. But now a peculiar
thing happened. The commissioners to survey and
mark the new boundary performed their work in May,
1771. The party included a group of Cherokee chiefs,
Stuart's deputy, Alexander Cameron, and a surveyor,
Colonel John Donelson, representing Virginia. The
man last named, the future father-in-law of Andrew
Jackson, now plays an interesting role. He finished his
survey and turned in his map and field notes to Lord
Dunmore, the new governor of Virginia. Dunmore in
March, 1772, transmitted them to Hillsborough with
the comment that the line surveyed was quite different
from that agreed upon in that it followed the Louisa
River to the Ohio and thus secured from the Indians a
large area beyond the treaty line.[6] He explained that
the Indians themselves had proposed it because of the
difficulties of running the line across mountainous
country to the Kanawha, and he emphasized the advantages of a natural river boundary.

Hillsborough replied expressing his astonishment
but reserving further comment. Stuart in the meantime
had been in Mobile and Pensacola, and he did not return until the spring of 1772. On February 25, 1773,
he wrote to Dartmouth, the new Colonial Secretary,
enclosing a map and field notes, and explaining the

variation in much the same fashion as had Dunmore. He identified the Louisa River in this way: "What a Coll. Donalson the Virginia Surveyour calls Louisa River in his report, and which forms the present boundary, is in Mitchell's map called Catawba or Cuttawa [the present Kentucky River]." This interpretation would of course throw a vast new territory into possession of the whites, and it was not long before it was generally accepted that the line surveyed was the Kentucky River. Historians, as well, have usually followed this assumption. Professor Alvord, however, in his *Mississippi Valley in British Politics,* rejects the theory that Donelson descended the Kentucky, and thinks that impression to have had an erroneous start from Stuart's letter to Dartmouth. He maintains that Donelson's Louisa River is the one originally so named by Dr. Thomas Walker on his memorable trip of 1750, and flowing into the Sandy River. As a matter of fact, practically all the mapmakers of Donelson's time seem to have given the name Louisa to a river flowing into the Kanawha or its tributary the Cole. I know of no mapmaker prior to 1771 who called the Kentucky the Louisa. But the conjectures of Professor Alvord and the uncertainty of others on this subject are based on the assumption that the map and field notes are lost. Alvord states that unavailing search had been made for these manuscripts which would, of course, settle the question.

The map and the field notes are in the library of the

Colonial Office in London.[8] The map itself is crude but clear and the notes are specific. They do settle the question. The line very evidently did run northwesterly to the Kentucky and down it to the Ohio. Furthermore, the field notes when worked out on modern geological survey maps show clearly a course leading to the upper waters of the Kentucky. In addition, letters from Alexander Cameron and from the Cherokees indicate that Colonel Donelson offered presents to the amount of £500 to be paid by Virginia in exchange for this enlargement, and that as late as 1775 this compensation had not been made.[9]

It is interesting to note that the Walker and Lewis map, by this time presumably reposing safely in a governmental office in London, was tampered with in connection with the new line. Some individual with blacker ink and a quite different hand traced out on the manuscript map a new line for the Ohio, retraced the Kentucky River, added the legend "Louisa Great River," and dotted in the survey line running southeast to the Holston.

Let us turn now from Virginia to other breaks in the line. Brief mention must suffice. At a congress at Augusta with the Cherokee and Creek Indians on June 1, 1773, two considerable tracts of land, known as the "traders' grant," were ceded by the Indians in return for a release from the heavy debts which they owed to the local traders, and which the British government now assumed. Two maps illustrate this "traders' grant." One, a large map four feet square, was sent to England by Stuart in his letter of June 13, 1772, when the cession was still only in contemplation. The other, entitled "A Map of the Lands ceded to his Majesty by the Creek and Cherokee Indians at a Congress held in Augusta . . . in June, 1773 by his Excellency Sir James Wright . . . and John Stuart Esq. . . . ," was "delineated" by Philip Yonge.[10]

Another alteration of the line concerned West Florida, where the line granted by the Creeks as a boundary back of the province in 1765 and extending as far west as the Alabama River has always baffled historians, at first because the treaty existed only in manuscript and had not been found by the writers on the subject. But even when the text of the treaty was located, the boundary clause was so badly worded as to make it seemingly impossible to identify. So competent a student of the region as Peter J. Hamilton printed the text in his *Colonial Mobile* (rev. ed., 1910) and attempted an identification. He pronounced it a difficult task, and his conclusions as to the location of the line are in a large part wrong. The solution is to be found partly in a description of the 1765 boundary which Stuart gave at a later treaty with the Creeks in 1771 (of which Hamilton makes no mention and presumably was unaware), and more definitely by a map in the Public Record Office in London. This map was made on rather flimsy paper, has been folded many times, and in places is crumbling to pieces. It was made for Stuart by David Tait in 1771.[11]

On it he marks the 1765 boundary with great clearness and also describes it in his annotations. This line was superseded at the congress which, as just mentioned, Stuart held with the Creeks in 1771, at Pensacola. The new line is described on the Tait map and also on an unsigned map, approximately four by six feet in size, sent to Hillsborough in July, 1772.[12]

Lastly, in 1777 Stuart held a council with the Choctaws and Chickasaws, largely in the interest of their allegiance to England against the revolting colonies. At this congress the Choctaws drew a line south from the mouth of the Yazoo River toward the coast, and then east until it met the Pascagoola River, and ceded any rights they might have to lands west of it (the so-called Natchez district), and to the south, parallel with the coast. This is the last boundary change made by Stuart, and the map made two years later by Joseph Purcell, his surveyor, adds the last section in the delineation of the line begun in 1763.[13]

Since the present writer has uncovered various so-called "lost maps," it seems to him no more than fair that he, as well, should complain of a "lost map" and thus leave for some other individual a similar opportunity for the sweet satisfaction of discovery. The map which Stuart, in his letter to Dartmouth of February 25, 1773, mentioned that he was enclosing to show Donelson's variation from the Lochaber Treaty line has not yet come to light. The known map by Donelson can be identified as the one coming from Dunmore;

Stuart's has not been found. Stuart adds that he is also marking on the map the bounds of the new government on the Ohio (i.e., Vandalia), which is an indication that the map was more extensive in scope than Donelson's. In reply Dartmouth says, "The map of North America will be of great use." This may be read as indicating its usefulness *when it should arrive,* but if it was actually sent it seems to have successfully hidden itself.

Some historians have identified this "lost map" of 1773 with Purcell's map of the Southern Indian District of 1776. This large map, more than five feet square, in the Library of the Colonial Office, is of considerable importance in its own right. It shows the entire southern department, the complete boundary line, and the limits of Vandalia.[14] But it is not the map of February, 1773, for it shows the completion of the "traders' grant," which was not made until July 1, 1773. Moreover, the Purcell map is clearly the one mentioned by Stuart in a letter to Lord George Germain in February, 1776, in which he wrote that he had promised such a map long ago for Lord Hillsborough. The details shown on it are correct for that date, even to the tentative drawing in of the Choctaw line subsequently agreed upon in 1777. In reporting the Choctaw conference Stuart says that the line agreed upon is identical with that which he laid down in the map submitted the year before, that is, 1776.

It may be worth noting that a duplicate of the Purcell map in the Library of the Colonial Office exists, as the writer was astonished to find some time ago, in the Newberry Library. It had been bought in England, and is very evidently an original. Which was copied from the other it is difficult to say, but the indications point to the Newberry copy as the earlier. This conclusion is drawn partly from the fact of slightly fuller detail, but also from the indication of the boundary line. The lines are identical, but the color of ink used, indicating sections surveyed, as compared with those merely agreed upon, gives a possible clue to priority.

These two maps (the Purcell map of 1776 and the Newberry Library's duplicate) give a most excellent summary of the complete boundary line as drawn by Stuart and also present a survey of the entire Indian distribution south of the Ohio. When supplemented by the nearly twenty other contemporaneous manuscript maps, they leave no part of the southern Indian boundary line which cannot be clearly located.

NOTES

[N.B.: This paper was originally read at the meeting of the American Historical Association in December, 1928. Photostats of a number of the maps which it mentions exist in the author's collection of manuscripts, now preserved in the Library of the University of California, Los Angeles. Much further work would undoubtedly have been done on it by the author before he published it, but it nevertheless seems best to publish it substantially as he left it because of the valuable information which it contains for specialists in this difficult field. A few small additions and alterations have been made to explain statements, and citations for the maps have been added from the author's collection.]

[1] Preserved loose in the Public Record Office, Colonial Office papers, Class 5, Vol. 65 (hereafter cited as C.O. 5/65, etc.)

[2] C.O. 5/69, p. 173: Report of March 7, 1768.

[3] Letter in Draper Collection (2 QQ 106) in the Wisconsin State Historical Society library.

[4] The report of Walker and Lewis to Botetourt, December 14, 1768, and the map were sent by Botetourt to Hillsborough, December 24, 1768, C.O. 5/1347, pp. 59 f.

[5] Shown on map in C.O. 5/72, p. 675.

[6] C.O. 5/1350, pp. 37–41.

[7] C.O. 5/74, pp. 123–125.

[8] Library of Colonial Office, North American Collection, Virginia, No. 19: the maps in this library were transferred to the Public Record Office in 1935.

[9] C.O. 5/76, pp. 181–184, 185–188.

[10] For the first map see C.O. 5/73, p. 321; for the second, C.O. 5/662, p. 133.

[11] C.O. 5/73, following p. 102.

[12] It has not been possible to locate the whereabouts of this map from Dr. Parish's notes.

[13] Lib. Col. Office, N. Amer. Col., Florida, No. 56: this map was completed in 1779.

[14] Lib. Col. Office, N. Amer. Col., General, No. 12.

EDMOND ATKIN, BRITISH
SUPERINTENDENT OF
INDIAN AFFAIRS

⸙

IN 1756, when the British government began to re-
organize its Indian policy in America on an imperial
basis, it appointed two superintendents of Indian affairs, one for the north and one for the south. Sir William Johnson, noted for his efficient management of
Iroquois affairs, was appointed for the northern district. The choice for the southern district was Edmond
Atkin. Little known at the time of his appointment,
he served during five years of the French and Indian
War, made a rather dismal failure in the office, and
dropped almost completely out of the knowledge of the
historians of succeeding generations.

The questions arise: Who was Edmond Atkin? Why
was he chosen for this important post? What were the
reasons for his comparative failure? And why, after occupying so high an office at so critical a time, has he remained in such comparative obscurity?

The lack of present-day information is partly due to
the paucity of readily available records. There is not to
be found in the British Public Record Office any such

accumulation of letters as came from Sir William Johnson or from Atkin's own successor, Captain John Stuart.
The data must be searched for in out-of-the-way corners
of the Public Record Office and the British Museum,
in the unprinted archives of South Carolina, and in
the widely scattered records of officials who retained
their public papers as private possessions. In the papers
of Lord Loudoun and General Abercrombie—now at
the Huntington Library—are a large number of letters
and other Atkin manuscripts, including one document
of unusual proportions (about 33,000 words) and of
considerable significance in connection with the development of an imperial Indian policy. It consists of
a letter by Atkin to the Earl of Halifax, President of
the Board of Trade, presenting in well-organized form
and with an impressive array of facts an account of the
Indian relations in the colonies, particularly in the
south, an arraignment of the current system of administration, a constructive analysis of needs, and a comprehensive, well-rounded plan for the administration of
Indian affairs. Doubtless it was this document, presented to Halifax in May, 1755, in response to a request
from the Board of Trade, that brought about Atkin's
appointment the following year as Superintendent of
Indian Affairs for the Southern Department. And it is
the content and significance of this manuscript that to
a large degree furnishes the justification for the present
paper.

Before studying Atkin's career as Indian agent or

even trying to appraise his report to Halifax, it is necessary to note some of the facts of his earlier life. He
himself said once in an Indian conference. "I am an
Englishman. I have lived almost ever since I was a boy
in South Carolina." In the 1730's, and for many years
afterward, he was a merchant in Charleston. The financial reports giving details of tax figures show the firm
of John Atkin and Company, as early as 1731, doing a
considerable business in sundry goods and merchan-
dise from England and the West Indies and in the exportation of colonial products, particularly deerskins
and sole leather. Edmond Atkin probably constituted
the "Company" in this firm. By 1735 the firm name had
become John and Edmond Atkin, and thereafter tax
lists, auction sales, advertisements of goods, and grants
of land show the activities of the partnership. In a six
months' period in the years 1735–1736 they imported
more than 10,000 gallons of rum, designed, the official
report states, "for the use of the colony of Georgia."

In 1738 Edmond Atkin was appointed by the King
a member of the Council of South Carolina, and this
position he retained for over twenty years. In his life
as a merchant dealing with the exportation of hides and
leather he inevitably came into close relationship with
the Indian traders, who no doubt bought his merchan-
dise and sold him the deerskins in exchange, and in his
position as a member of the Council he had ample opportunity to get a clear picture of Indian relations from
the viewpoint of a public official. The journals of the

Council are full of debates over Indian affairs, depositions from traders, and reports of agents, and in the council hall over and over again the Indian visitors themselves appeared.

In 1746 occurred what is known as the Choctaw Revolt, led by Red Shoe or Soulier Rouge, who brought most of the Choctaw tribes over to the side of the English. Atkin became very much interested in this episode in the international rivalry over the Choctaws, and a few years later, while in London, wrote what he termed "An Historical Account of the Choctaw Revolt," a document scarcely less formidable than his report to Halifax. There is no time here to do more than say that, in spite of the confusion of details in which he becomes entangled, it is a mine of information on the Choctaw Indians, the intrigues of traders, and the ways of colonial politics. Neither James Adair, author of *The History of the American Indians,* nor Governor Glen of South Carolina gets a clean bill of health in this *petite histoire* of the Indian trade.

In 1750 Atkin sold his goods at auction and left for England, where he stayed for six years—without, however, giving up his place on the South Carolina Council. He lived in Craven Street, was occasionally seen at social affairs, and produced the documents mentioned— the account of the Choctaw Revolt and the treatise on Indian affairs. The latter—much the more able paper of the two—was penned in 1754 and delivered to Halifax on May 20, 1755. A brief summary of its contents is now essential.

Atkin begins by pointing out the wretched situation resulting in America from the current system of administering Indian affairs and the immediate need of change. He comments extendedly on the designs and operations of the French in America, their unity of administration, their forts, and their constant efforts to gain the affections of the Indians. He notes particularly their provision for gunsmiths among the tribes, and their very careful discrimination and wisdom in the distribution of presents and ammunition. He then discusses in some detail the various policies of supervision carried on by the English colonies. The inadequacies of the laws themselves and the prevalent abuses are clearly portrayed. A very important section follows in which he describes the situation, the character, and the disposition of the Indian nations. Devoting only a comparatively few pages to the northern Indians, he goes into extended discussion of the Catawbas, Cherokees, Creeks, Chickasaws, and Choctaws. Details of their numbers and their fighting strength, their traits and their policies, their disposition toward other Indians, toward the English and toward the French, and their attitude toward forts, trade, rum, and ammunition, illustrate the range of Atkin's observations.

Finally he presents a "Plan of a General Direction and Management of the Indian Affairs throughout North America," so detailed that it permits only the mention here of its most important points. It involved the King's taking under his immediate direction whatever concerned the Indians, and dividing the nations into two districts. The northern district was to comprise the Six Nations with their dependents; the southern was to include particularly the Cherokees, Catawbas, Creeks, Chickasaws, and Choctaws.

Over these two divisions were to be two imperial officers—superintendents or commissioners—who were to make new treaties with each of the Indian nations. These new treaties were to require from the Indians that they traffic with no other Europeans but the English, that they admit to their villages as English traders only those having a license, that they come not into the plantations or settlements without leave from the Governor, that they do their utmost to prevent or give satisfaction for violence, that they "treat all our friends as their friends and all our enemies as their enemies," and that they do not sell their lands to any of the King's subjects, but to His Majesty only.

On the part of the English the treaties were to provide that a fort or blockhouse be built in every nation desiring it, that their guns and hatchets be mended there gratis, that they be supplied with goods on moderate terms fixed between them and the traders, and that they be visited by the commissioner each year for the hearing of complaints against traders and for the promotion of friendship.

Atkin's plan set up the two commissioners as independent of any particular governor or provincial authority and vested in them the command of all forts and garrisons in the Indian country. The commissioner on his annual visitation to each nation, or in general conferences, was to be accompanied by a person deputed by each governor involved. The commissioners and their provincial deputies, and others in the Indian service, were to be barred from any participation in the Indian trade directly or indirectly.

The scheme also provided for a King's engineer to be sent with each commissioner to make choice of sites and to build the forts. Troops were to be increased to give adequate garrison forces. An interpreter, a gunsmith, and a missionary ("not very young") from the Society for the Propagation of the Gospel were to be provided for each fort. Each of the commissioners was to have a troop of rangers to patrol the back of the settlements (and these might have dogs with them "the more effectually to discover skulking Indians by their scent"). A secretary was also to be provided for the use of each commissioner.

Thereafter followed explicit directions for the licensing and control of traders, the distribution of presents, and the use of rum. A Parliamentary act was involved in his plan, in order to unify and enforce the new system and to establish a General Provincial Fund for the service of all the colonies by their respective governments.

In addition to these provisions, he stated other objects to be pursued, including the destruction of French forts; the securing, by means of forts, of the navigation of the Great Lakes; the possession of the Tennessee River, which was to separate the two districts; and the control of the mouth of the Appalachicola River; and finally, the formation of a union among the southern nations similar to that of the Iroquois.

It is well to pause here and note the tendency of official opinion in regard to the control of Indian affairs at this time. The traditional policy had been to allow each colony to handle its own Indian problem, sometimes through the governor and his council, sometimes with the use of an Indian agent or Board of Commissioners acting for the colony. This had been attended with much graft because of the frequent participation of the agents in the Indian trade, and the uncontrolled abuses perpetrated by the traders in the Indian country. Still more fundamentally harmful, perhaps, was the effect upon the Indians of the rivalries of the representatives of the various colonies, who blocked each other's moves, told different stories to the same Indians, and destroyed any impression of unity.

A tendency toward a more unified policy is found in the instructions given to Governor Osborn of New York in 1753 in connection with the coming meeting of colonial representatives at Albany. When the Albany Congress met in 1754, it went so far as to draw up a plan recommending the control of Indian affairs by a president general and his council of commissioners from the various colonies. But the Board of Trade was interested in an imperial control rather than a single colonial control. Halifax, then president of the Board, wrote in April, 1754, to the Secretary of State suggesting a line of forts in the Indian country and two general commissioners with separate districts to visit the forts, control the deputies, distribute Indian presents, and hold conferences. In August the Board of Trade drew up a report urging further centralization by the appointment of a commander-in-chief of all forts and troops in the American colonies, who should also be commissary general for Indian affairs, and the provision for maintaining commissaries in such forts as should be thought proper.

The result of this kind of discussion, stimulated by the outbreak of war in America, was the appointment of General Braddock, who was to go with an army to America as commander-in-chief with authority to appoint William Johnson as Superintendent of Indian Affairs in the northern colonies and to take steps to find a suitable man to fill a corresponding position in the southern colonies. Braddock arrived in America, appointed Johnson, failed to do anything about a southern superintendent, and died on the field of battle in July, 1755. It was just before this disaster that the report of Atkin came to the attention of Halifax and the Board of Trade.

The proposals of Atkin were not altogether new. The writings of Benjamin Franklin and Thomas Pownall, William Johnson, Peter Wraxall, and the Earl of Halifax all suggest features of Atkin's plan. But none of these did more than make suggestions. Atkin's report worked the whole group of new ideas into a complete scheme, and if, as he himself states, it was written in 1754, it is not only the most complete, but also one of the very earliest.

The plan, however, was not without practical defects. The provision for two imperial superintendents, without a superior officer in America, ran counter to a growing desire of the British government to put a military commander-in-chief in the colonies and give him, in addition to his military duties, the supervision of Indian affairs.

The multiplicity of officers and attending troops under Atkin's scheme may have been desirable, but it outran the funds which the government thought necessary for the purpose. In general the plan involved too thoroughgoing and sudden a reorganization of Indian affairs.

Evidently the document was impressive enough, however, both in its display of knowledge of the southern Indians and in the definiteness of its plan, to convince the Board of Trade of the fitness of Atkin for one of the superintendencies. In January, 1756, the Board decided to name a new commander-in-chief with extraordinary powers and to appoint Sir William Johnson as superintendent for the northern district and Edmond Atkin for the southern. Atkin's commission bore the date of May 14, 1756.

But Atkin did not find himself embarked on smooth

seas. In June he appeared before the Board of Trade pleading for instructions, and was told that they had insufficient information and could give him none. He must rely upon Lord Loudoun, who as commander-in-chief would give him instructions when he should arrive in America. Atkin reached New York October 6. He had a conference with Loudoun and Johnson, made additional recommendations as to Indian affairs, and participated with Johnson in an Indian conference at Fort Johnson in an endeavor to bring the Iroquois into friendly relations with the southern nations. He then returned to New York and followed Loudoun to Boston in an unsuccessful plea for instructions, drawing up a sample of his own for approval. On March 1, 1757, he was in New York, writing despairingly to England about the situation.

He accompanied Loudoun to Philadelphia on the same quest. There he finally received at least verbal instructions, and then moved south to Virginia, where his real work began. He tried unavailingly to get the legislature of Virginia to enact proper laws for the regulation of the Indian trade. A considerable number of Cherokees were gathered in western Virginia and required attention. He repaired to Winchester at the suggestion of Governor Dinwiddie, who for a time washed his hands of Indian matters and wrote to Colonel George Washington that the latter was no longer to have concern with Indian affairs since Atkin was appointed for that purpose. After a few months, Atkin appointed Christopher Gist as deputy for this region and journeyed on southward, arriving at Charleston, South Carolina, March 23, 1758.

Here he made the tactical blunder of allowing William Byrd III, an emissary sent out by Governor Dinwiddie, to act in his place in negotiations with the Cherokees.

Atkin himself officiated as president of the Council of South Carolina from June to September, and then set off to the country of the Creeks, where he spent many months holding conferences and negotiating treaties with the Creeks and the Choctaws. He nearly lost his life in October, 1759, when, in the midst of a conference, a Creek Indian felled him with his tomahawk.

By the end of March, 1760, he was back again in Charleston, writing at length to Pitt and drawing up a statement of his accounts. Meanwhile a most critical situation had been developing at Fort Loudoun, built by the South Carolinians in the Overhill country of the Cherokees. The garrison was finally massacred and the only surviving officer was Captain John Stuart, Atkin's successor in office. Atkin was criticized vigorously for not having turned his attention more definitely to allaying hostility among the Cherokees in this region. So far as the writer has been able to determine, he penetrated no farther into the Cherokee country than Fort Prince George, where the *South Carolina Gazette* of July 5, 1759, reports him to have been, in company with a number of wounded officers. He died on October 8, 1761, at Mar's Bluff, in Craven County.

The failure of his superintendency rests largely upon Atkin himself. He was lacking in executive ability, slow and vacillating in action, unwilling to undertake difficult enterprises without thorough equipment and funds, and was evidently wanting in personality and tact. In addition, he was in ill health most of the time of his service. But other reasons for his futility must also be considered. The British government was unwilling to go the whole way in his support. Loudoun, among whose papers Atkin's report to Halifax is found, was distinctly indifferent to him, possibly influenced by the fact that Atkin had contemplated no subordination to a commander-in-chief. Johnson did not give him the most complete coöperation. Loudoun himself stated that although John Pownall had sent over presents to be divided between the districts in the proportion of two-thirds for the southern district and one-third for the northern, Johnson had persuaded Loudoun to reverse the ratio, on the theory that the crisis was occurring principally in the north. The governors, though directed by the Board of Trade to coöperate with Atkin, soon slipped back into the ways of separate colonial action regardless of Atkin; the legislatures were unready to enact laws conforming to his ideas, and naturally enough the traders opposed him with the utmost vigor. At an unusually critical time, and after six years' absence from the country, he faced a task greater than that of Johnson, who had a smaller territory, fewer tribes, and fewer colonial officers to combat.

Finally, it must be said that the time was not ripe for so thoroughgoing a change as the one which Atkin proposed and clung to so tenaciously. Real administration of such a plan was not attempted until 1764, when the French had withdrawn from America. The imperial gains made at this time were in part given up again in 1768, and with the coming of the American Revolution the Indian administration became largely a matter of opportunism.

In conclusion, it is only fair to say that the failure of Edmond Atkin as Superintendent of Indian Affairs does not in any way vitiate the contribution which he made in his report to Halifax in 1755. Upon that must rest his claim to recognition. As a historical narrative and description of the southern Indians it is unequaled in its time. It is less full than James Adair's *History of the American Indians,* but it comprises a much more definitely organized account and antedates Adair's work by twenty years. Moreover, it presents a new policy of Indian administration, more comprehensive and detailed than that of any of his contemporaries, or of any of his followers for many years to come.

BY SEA TO CALIFORNIA

───────────────── ◄ ❧ ► ─────────────────

FROM THE TIME when men first went down to
the sea in ships until comparatively recent years
there have been but the two modes of travel: overland
journeying and voyaging by sea. Two legs might carry
one to near-by places, and by dint of great energy to
far-off haunts, as witness Cabeza de Vaca. But the process was slow, plebeian, and uninviting; and the sub-
stitution of four legs for two only moderately relieved
the tedium. There was a touch of aristocracy about sea-
faring, for the comparative ease of such wandering was
attained only when an outlay was made for a boat, and
also for supplies, since game did not spring up along
the pathway of the sea, nor nourishing berries grow on
the waves.

Given this initial equipment, the sailor had a distinct advantage. The roadways of the ocean covered
three-quarters of the surface of the globe, and unbroken
water routes led him to the most distant shores. Thus
Cabrillo reached Alta California two centuries before
Junípero Serra; Francis Drake was coasting the northwest shoreline before his countrymen had even begun
the long land trail across the continent; James Cook
visited the Canadian coast before Mackenzie reached it

overland; Captain Gray entered the mouth of the Columbia River a decade ahead of Lewis and Clark; and
when Jedediah Smith, ragged and footsore, made his
way across the deserts and mountains to southern California, he found at San Diego American ship captains
who had so established themselves as to be able to rescue him from the hands of the Mexican governor.

The advantages and disadvantages of sea travel to
California in the gold days as compared with those of
land travel seem worthy of attention. There were differences more significant than the superficial ones of
speed and expense and numbers. The conditions of
travel and their effects upon the travelers; the personnel in each case and the results in the history of California; the routes and points along the way and their
relation to international affairs and to the conquest of
the continent—all these demand our notice if we are
interested in anything more than a picturesque impression of gold seekers on the move.

When gold was discovered in California in January,
1848, the earliest result was, naturally enough, an influx of fortune hunters from the neighboring land area.
San Francisco and Monterey were almost deserted, and
soon came a stream of adventurers from the towns farther south. But this was only a local manifestation. The
world at large—even the adjoining territory of Oregon—was still unaware of the discovery. The news
spread, however, with the passing to and fro of ships.
The Hawaiian Islands received the tidings in June,

1848, and by July gold hunters from the Islands were crowding the boats bound for San Francisco. The word was carried by sea from Hawaii to Oregon, and a few men with pack animals reached the mines in September. In the late summer Peter H. Burnett, who became the first American governor of California, led out a considerable band of Oregonians overland by wagon train to the goldfields. And the brig *Henry* gathered together its travelers at Oregon City and sailed down the coast, arriving in September ahead of Burnett and his landsmen.

In this same month of September, Colonel Mason's messenger, Loeser, on his way to deliver the official report to the President at Washington, touched at Payta on the coast of Peru, and straightway from the ports of Peru and Chile ships set sail for El Dorado. Passing on by way of Panama to Washington, the messenger reached the capital in time for his report to be incorporated with President Polk's message to Congress on December 5, 1848. This presentation of the case, broadcast by the eastern newspapers and supported by nuggets of gold which Loeser had brought, crystallized the excitement which had been growing ever since the first rumors had come in September.

To cross the continent would not be possible until the winter was over, but there were the ships; and craft of all descriptions, many of them scarcely seaworthy, were hauled out and crowded with prospective miners eager to be on their way round the Horn. In the towns of

New England and New York, men organized into companies, bought old hulks, tumbled aboard, and set sail. Philadelphia, Baltimore, and Charleston added their quota to the fleet. The sea trail of the American forty-niners had begun.

With most of the adventurers speed was the great consideration, and many sought to substitute for the long trip round the Horn a double sea passage with a land crossing at Panama. By a fortuitous happening the United States government had, in the year 1848, made contracts for the carrying of the mail by steamer from New York to Chagres on the Atlantic side of the Isthmus of Panama and from Panama on the Pacific side to Oregon and California. The Pacific Mail Steamship Company provided three side-wheel steamers, the *California,* the *Oregon,* and the *Panama,* and on October 6, 1848, the *California* left New York to round Cape Horn and take up its duties in the Pacific service. At the time of its departure mining interest had not yet been aroused in the East and the ship carried no gold seekers. But when it reached Callao, Peru, in December, it found a gold-mad throng of South Americans clamoring for passage to the mines. The captain took aboard fifty or seventy-five passengers and continued north toward Panama. Meanwhile the *Falcon,* a steamer in the Atlantic service, had left New York for the Isthmus to connect with the *California.* Its sailing date, December 1, was before the peak of the gold fever and it had few passengers for California. But it touched at

New Orleans and here two hundred excited fortune hunters were given accommodations. They arrived at Chagres December 26, crossed the Isthmus, and impatiently waited for the coming of the *California*. The latter boat did not appear for more than a month, during which time newcomers crossed the ridge and dropped down to the village of Panama to wait for passage. On January 9, 1849, according to a report in the *New York Tribune,* there were four hundred and fifty passengers on the Isthmus. When the *California* finally arrived, on January 30, there were many hundreds more, all determined to embark. Already some, unwilling to wait, had set out in decrepit old boats, and even in log canoes, and some essayed to go by land from Panama up the coast to the mines. The *California* had accommodations for one hundred. It took aboard more than four hundred persons and sailed on to San Francisco, where amid great excitement it arrived on February 28, 1849. Thus came the first Argonauts from the United States to the goldfields of California. On April first the *Oregon* arrived after a still wilder struggle at the Isthmus and, early in June, came the *Panama*. Brigs and barks, pilot boats and clipper ships began to drift in from round the Horn. The proverbial forest of masts appeared in San Francisco Bay while passengers, and often officers and crew as well, hurried ashore to make their fortunes.

Where were the overland immigrants while these boats were arriving? In February, when the *California* reached port, the landsmen were still manfully and prosaically fighting winter in their own homes. By April, when the *Oregon* arrived, they were gathering at Independence or at other points along the crook of the Missouri, where the trails started. In May they were under way, for the grass on the plains was now high enough for food for their animals. In July they began to arrive at the mines and soon their name was legion. It is thus evident that many shiploads of adventurers were already at work in the goldfields before the caravans of overland travelers reached California.

Although they were a little late, the landsmen had certain very definite advantages. The trail across the continent was of such grueling difficulty that those who were unfit were largely weeded out. Scurvy and dysentery took their toll. Cholera was rampant in 1849 and proved a still greater scourge. Thirst and hunger, too much rain and too much sun, the long miles on the plains and the high miles in the mountains defeated all too many of them. But the fit survived and reached the mines ready for immediate and active participation in the life of hardship and physical and mental strain.

Let us contemplate in comparison the life on board a sailing vessel making the trip round the Horn. Just how fitting a preparation was it for the life of a miner? It was by no means free from hardship, suffering, and danger. But in spite of seasickness and scurvy, bad storm and poor craft, unfit food or short rations, there were few fatalities. Now and then a man fell overboard or died of disease. But those solemn occasions when the ship's company stood by the rail while a body, wrapped in a sailcloth and attached to a weighted plank, was slipped into the unrecording sea, were unusual events in a voyage. Compare on the other hand such oft-repeated entries in overland journals as: "Passed 13 graves today," or "Today Mr. Parker was buried beside Mr. Boyden," or "Mr. Jones was taken in the morning with cholera and died at three o'clock."

On board ship, between storms and other discomforts there were long days of tranquillity, of peaceful reading for some, of ennui for others, allayed by preaching or gambling, by the issuing of ship newspapers and the making of tents, by lyceums and pranks and quarrels. On one ship was a man who entertained his fellows by playing the violin or singing snatches of opera, and when these efforts failed to charm, he gave them more permanent joy by tattooing appropriate designs upon their arms and chests.

An unpublished manuscript at the Huntington Library, the journal of William D. Herbert, gives a view of life on board the *Elvira,* which sailed from Boston on the second of January, 1849, and reached San Francisco in the latter part of June. A stop for repairs—the only one on the trip—gave them two diverting weeks at Rio de Janeiro. Frequently on the Atlantic they spoke other ships and sometimes raced with them. "Humbugging off Cape Horn," as he expressed it, they experienced the usual storms. Herbert interspersed poetry throughout his journal, but on April 3 he remarked: "There is no poetry off Cape Horn. Chilblains are the general complaint of all hands and the cabin is preferred at present to the deck. We now think of touching at the Sandwich Islands for water." But rain fell on the twenty-second and, caught in a sailcloth, it made a stop unnecessary.

Food seems to have been excellent. On April 24 all hands were weighed and Herbert remarked, "We all seem to gain on this voyage." His own gain must have been quite perceptible, for he records that he weighed one hundred and thirty-five pounds before leaving Boston, one hundred and forty-four just before getting to Rio, and now tipped the scales at one hundred and fifty-eight, a gain of twenty-three pounds. Some of their blessings, however, were departing ones. On April 30 he states, "Today water was allowanced—15 galls. for 23 persons for 24 hours." On June 12 he says, "This morning our butter gave out"; and the next day, "Our hen (last remnant of her race) in attempting to fly from the long boat to the deck was carried overboard." Three days later, "Killed the last of our pigs." But while he helped to exterminate the hens and the pigs, he also exhibited a devouring taste in literature. On May 5 he says, "Today finished the first volume of the history of England by Goldsmith"; and on June 7, "Today lost a volume of Byron over but obtained it again." Surely this man was fitting himself for other pursuits than the strenuous one of mining.

The fact is inescapable that the trip round the Horn

left the traveler with soft muscles and manifestly unprepared for the rigorous régime of the mines. For many, the sudden change from six or eight months of idleness to extreme physical exertion proved fatal.

An examination of the personnel of land and sea companies brings interesting conclusions. Perhaps the largest proportion of land travelers came from the Middle West, which was at that time the frontier and predominantly agricultural. Thus the caravans brought men of independent spirit, accustomed to hardships and manual labor—an ideal group for successful mining operations. The ship passengers (though including some from the Middle West who descended the Mississippi and undertook a boat voyage rather than wait until the end of winter) nevertheless were recruited largely from the Atlantic seaboard and from foreign countries. Their original occupations were more varied and in general had less relation to mining. True, there were farmers from New England and New York, lumbermen from Maine, and whaling captains from the towns of Massachusetts, but there were also clerks and storekeepers by the thousands, newspapermen, lawyers and doctors, discontented teachers and preachers, jewelers and japanners, tailors and tinsmiths, printers and painters and peddlers, brass turners and piano makers and bonnet pressers. These came to San Francisco, and on finding that the mines were a considerable journey inland many of them ended by staying in town and remaining storekeepers and clerks, printers and painters and jewelers. The overland travelers dropped down from the Sierra into the mines and set at once to work.

Many, of course, came by sea with no intention of being miners. They realized the need of supporting occupations and prepared and equipped themselves accordingly. The landfarers could bring little baggage with them. The physical machinery of civilization which reached California in the 'fifties could not easily have been hauled or carted or carried across the plains and over the mountains before the advent of the railroad, but the seagoers were less handicapped and they brought cargoes of goods to sell, including everything from tacks to mining machinery. Their ships carried furniture and fixtures, printing presses and ready-cut houses, and even small steamboats destined to be set down in the harbor and to ply between the Bay and the mines. Many a sailing vessel which brought gold seekers was converted into a storeship or prison ship or a rooming house.

It would doubtless be unfair to say that the landsmen came with brawn and the seafarers with brains, yet the diversity of talent, political, financial, industrial, literary and commercial, that came in ships to our western shores cannot be overlooked. The California State Constitutional Convention of 1849 consisted of forty-eight members. Six were native Californians. Of seven I have found no account to tell how they came. Twelve have been recorded as coming overland, and at least twenty-three are known to have come by sea. The first mayors of San Francisco and Monterey came by sea, as did one of the first two United States Senators, at least one of the first two Congressmen, and Judge Stephen Fields, later a member of the United States Supreme Court. The seafarers built up mercantile establishments in San Francisco and Sacramento and Marysville, sometimes operating through the same company formation as that in which they made the sea voyage, as did the Lady Adams Company of Sacramento. They became editors of the *Alta California* and other San Francisco newspapers. They entered politics and formed a large group in the first legislature—"the legislature of a thousand drinks." Without question, the cities felt their impress and the mining activities lived by reason of their support. Probably it should also be said that the ships brought in many rascals: professional gamblers, riffraff from eastern and European cities, and "Sydney Ducks" from Australia, who helped to make California lawless.

It is of course obvious that most of the foreign element in the mines and in the towns of California came by sea rather than by land. Hawaii and China, the Philippines and the Marquesas Islands, all sent early gold seekers. South Americans came with Latin enthusiasm. Australia and New Zealand sent many a boatload of none too desirable characters. The European countries were touched with the gold fever nearly as soon as the American East.. In the *New York Tribune* for December 15, 1849, appears the following item from San Francisco: "Foreign flags in the harbor: English, French, Portuguese, Italian, Hamburgh, Bremen, Belgium, New Granadian, Dutch, Swedish, Oldenburgh, Chilean, Peruvian, Russian, Mexican, Ecuadorian, Hanoverian, Norwegian, Hawaiian, and Tahitian." The effect of all this foreign influx in creating a cosmopolitan state can readily be appreciated.

The land routes to the mines were numerous, and so were the routes by sea. The voyage round the Horn was sometimes made without a break, but usually there were several stops. Each ship took its own course. In most cases Rio de Janeiro was visited, often for several days or weeks. Sometimes Santa Catarina Island, farther down the coast, was part of the itinerary. At the southern end of the continent three ways presented themselves. The Strait of Magellan was dangerous for large ships and presented hazards for any, but it shortened the distance and offered a way of avoiding the storms for which Cape Horn was famous. Another possibility was Le Maire Strait, lying farther east between Tierra del Fuego and Staten Island. The *Elvira* attempted to penetrate this passage, but, like many another ship, found a heavy head wind at the mouth, and the captain decided to go round Staten Island instead.

Rounding Cape Horn was more dreaded than any other part of the trip. Storms were particularly severe and ships often spent months in getting round the tip of the continent. The island of Juan Fernandez, famous

to voyagers as "Robinson Crusoe's Island," was sometimes visited after the Horn was passed. Valdivia and
Valparaiso on the Chilean coast and the Peruvian port
of Callao were more frequent stops.

The Horn trip was bound to be long. The ordinary
sailing vessels—and these carried the great proportion
of the Argonauts—took from five to eight months. The
clipper ships made better time and reduced the passage
to as low as eighty-nine days. Even this seemed long to
the impatient ones, and many combined sea voyages
with a land crossing in the interest of speed. The most
popular crossing at first was at Panama. If all went
perfectly (which seldom happened), Chagres could be
reached in about nine days. The Isthmus could be
traversed in two or three days more, and if a boat
chanced to be waiting on the Pacific side one could be
in San Francisco in little more than a month. Needless
to say, such a schedule was rare. In the course of time
Nicaragua eclipsed Panama in popularity, since it cut
many hundred miles from the journey from New York
to San Francisco. Probably the most discouraging combination was one involving a land trip across Mexico.
Voyagers came by boat to Corpus Christi in Texas or to
Vera Cruz on the Mexican coast, and blithely attempted
to reach Mazatlan or some other Pacific port. They
usually experienced all the disadvantages and hardships of both land and sea travel and fervently warned
their friends back home to take any route rather than
this.

Joseph McGaffey, leaving Boston March first, approached Corpus Christi and entered this remark in his journal: "We shall be rejoiced when we exchange the old vessel for a comfortable seat on a horse or a jackass." But the long trip across Texas and Mexico must have made him wish oftentimes for the "old vessel." After traveling overland for weeks and losing most of his friends by cholera, he reached Mazatlan and found passage on a boat which landed him at Santa Barbara. From here he was forced to go overland to the mines, where soon after his arrival he died as a result of his exposure and hardships.

A company known as the New England Pioneers had a varied experience. They went by rail from Boston via Charleston to New Orleans, and thence by boat to Vera Cruz. Traveling inland to Mexico City and across to San Blas, they again took ship to Mazatlán and transferred there to another boat which proved to be leaky and set them down at San Jose, Mexico. From there they traveled north by land taking fifty-one days from San Jose to San Diego.

Not all the seafarers rejoiced when they reached San Francisco. William De Costa, a printer, came on the *Duxbury* with the "Old Harvard Company of Cambridge." He closes his journal with these sardonic remarks: "At 9 a.m. opened the mouth of the harbor, came in sight of the shipping, and poking our jib boom through the forest of masts we came to anchor in front of the town at 12 m. We are to the end of our journey,

are in the promised land. Well, what of it? Thursday
and Friday saw the sights and on Saturday went to work
in the office of the *Pacific News*—intending by so doing
to realize a fortune in a few days."

A young man arriving in the *Leonore* on July 5,
wrote home: "Just arrived—San Francisco be damned!
further particulars in my next."

Yet it is safe to say that the gold fever burned at white
heat when the ships approached San Francisco. On its
first arrival, in February, 1849, the steamer *California*
was laid up for months because of the desertion of its
crew and all its officers save one engineer. The *Oregon*
took great precautions, but the ship carpenter was so
eager that he swam ashore at Monterey.

The ardor of many of the Argonauts cooled, however, and soon the returning boats were heavily laden.
Here again is a contrast with land travel. Without
doubt a much larger proportion of seacomers than of
landcomers returned to their homes. Especially is this
true of the foreigners. South Americans, Orientals, and
Europeans took to the sea again, sometimes with fortunes, but often disillusioned. Furthermore, the ships
carried thousands on the return trip who had come by
land. And they carried much gold. The *New York
Tribune* in January, 1849, reported that William G.
Marcy, son of the Secretary of War, had collected fifteen
barrels of "gold ore" which he had buried until a ship
should arrive. General Bennett Riley, in a probably
more authentic account, reported in February, from

Valparaiso, that the *Lexington* had arrived in that port with $350,000 worth of gold aboard.

It is hard to estimate the numbers that came by sea. The *New York Tribune* in February, 1849, made a careful list of boats and passengers sailing from eastern ports since December 7, 1848, and cast up a total of more than 8,000 passengers. This was for only about two months and took no account of foreign ports. The California *State Register* for 1857 gave the aggregate arrivals at the port of San Francisco from April, 1849, to the end of the year, as more than 91,000. Other sources gave a smaller total. But exact figures are immaterial. By any count the number of seacomers is extraordinary, and their influence, especially in the towns of California, of great importance.

There remains to be considered the effect of the two streams upon the conquest of the continent. In the opinion of the writer, the landfarers and not the seafarers made California a part of the nation. The Argonauts came home or wrote home to tell of adventures by the way—of jaunts at Rio and Valparaiso, of storms in rounding the Horn, and of exciting times at the Isthmus of Panama. And no doubt these contacts in foreign places had an effect on international relationships, and gave a stimulus to the project of an Isthmian canal. But what booted all these tales to growing America? The tales, however, of the lands that lay between the Mississippi and the Pacific, though these lands might be disfigured by deserts and wrinkled by mountain ranges and devastated by hostile Indians, served as a challenge and a guide to an advancing people. The bark and the brig, the clipper ship and the sidewheel steamer, brought the East to California, but the slow plodding oxen joined California indissolubly to the East.

In other words, the seagoers had less incidental value than the landsmen. The Argonauts themselves and their ships' cargoes were a very real contribution. Their pathway, however, was erased behind them. Almost it could be said: "They came like water and like wind they went." The wake of their vessels on the surface of the sea was stilled before the white sails dropped beyond the horizon. But the trails of the landsmen were marked with lasting mementos, at first only abandoned wagons and outfits, grim skeletons of oxen, the graves of unfortunate emigrants, and the trodden and wheel-cut line of advance. But these gave way to forts and towns, farms and fences, permanent roads, railways, land systems, and statehood. A nation was building out into the West, and it was the landsmen and not the seafarers who laid out the lines between the old and the new, the East and the West, and made sure that neither alkali nor altitude nor miles nor months should keep far-distant California from its manifest destiny as a part of the United States of America.

THE PACIFIC HISTORICAL
REVIEW

[AN EDITORIAL]

———— ⋅《 》⋅ ————

THE PACIFIC COAST through many genera-
tions was the far edge of the world for a people moving west. Balboa climbed over the mountains and found
it. Magellan discovered a passage by which ships could
reach it. Thereafter by land and sea men visited the
western shore of the continent. Conquistador and
priest, trader and pirate, rancher and miner and town
builder fashioned the rim of land into a place of legend
and a lure for the adventurous. Ships that beat their
way round the Horn, pack-trains that toiled across the
southern mountains, wagons whose creaking wheels
rolled over interminable miles of dust converted into
a part of America this farthest margin of expansion.

But its dwellers looked across the mountains to the
lands from which they had come. Their backs were to
the sea. The ocean behind them seemed at best but an
avenue by which ships could bring them news and supplies from the East. The sea was an empty room in the
dwelling place of mankind—a vacant space setting them
apart from an ancient and disregarded world. For the

most part the inhabitants of the Pacific Coast forgot
that the ocean itself was the scene and center of a great
history. They ceased to remember that Magellan, having found the water route to the Pacific, was killed in
battle in the Philippine Islands; that Captain Cook,
after visiting the Northwest Coast, was killed in the
Hawaiian Islands; that Chinese had probably crossed
the ocean to California long before the Europeans arrived; that Spanish galleons had plied back and forth
from Manila to the California and Mexican coasts before Jamestown was founded; that Kendrick and Robert Gray and other skippers carried Northwestern furs
to China and there bought Oriental goods for New
England consumption; that Oregon learned of gold in
California by way of Hawaii, and that Peruvians and
Australians beat the overland forty-niners into the
goldfields.

The Pacific Coast frontiersmen were engrossed with
their own task—the conquest and development of their
continent. But the time came when the struggle for
the possession of the West was finished. Railways sup-
planted the oxcart and the pack train. The movement
was westward, but it became less of a push and more of
a drift. The spirit was gone from it. They were a numerous people now. Material comforts had followed
them. Culture was finding its home among them. Less
often did they look back toward the East. They glanced
over their shoulders and saw Hawaii. They turned
about and there was an awakened Japan, a China with

its eternal problems, a Russia on the sea at the end of a transcontinental march like their own. The Pacific was no longer an empty room, a vacant space setting them apart from the Old East. It introduced them to a strange world. They had settled and tamed a land. Now they found themselves in the open doorway of a new life.

As America had been coming into equality with Europe, so was the Pacific coming into an equality with the Atlantic. The Atlantic brought an old world in touch with a new. The Pacific brought a new world in touch with an old. California and China, Oregon and Hawaii, Mexico and the Philippines, Peru and Australia made each other's acquaintance. They came to see that, instead of a dividing factor, a river or an ocean is bound to become a unifying force. The Basin of the Pacific was an entity. Its history was a unity. A community of interest and experience bound together the peoples that looked out upon the great ocean.

The *Pacific Historical Review* seeks to be a medium of expression for this unity. It will welcome articles on the western states of both North and South America, on the islands of the sea, and on the new and old countries of Australia and Japan, China, and Asiatic Russia. Its purpose is not so much to evaluate the present as to recount and interpret the story of the past, which has determined and produced the present. It does not endorse that which men say in its pages. It will, however, demand an honest historical purpose of its contributors, and competence in the investigation and presentation of their subjects.

Once a year there will be a departure from the field of the Pacific. For five years the Pacific Coast Branch has printed the *Proceedings* of its annual meetings. The *Proceedings* in that form will not for the present be published; but one number of the *Review,* probably the June number, will be devoted to the papers read at the annual meeting. Since these contributions are drawn from the whole field of history, the *Proceedings* number may at times seem to bear little resemblance to a regional journal. Yet those scholars who live in the West but study and love and teach us the lore of other lands should have their day in court. And the exotic flavor of an occasional article on George Washington, or Peter the Hermit, or Tiglathpileser may help to save the rest of us from the sin of provincialism.

THE WEST

·《 》·

LITERALLY a direction, more broadly and ade-
quately speaking a region, the West as a concept
in American history is much more than either: it is a
set of conditions obtaining and constantly changing in
the land beyond the settled East. It is distinct from the
Westward Movement since the latter term indicates a
process. The West is the *raison d'être* of the Westward
Movement. It is more than the frontier, since the frontier, or zone of the edge of settlement, was a local phenomenon. The West was the sum total, at any given
time, of the various zones of advance: the impermanent
activities of explorers, traders, and cattle rangers, the
frontier of settlement, and finally the conditions exist-
ing between the frontier and the East, where the rigors
of pioneering were partly overcome and the comforts
of life had in part penetrated. The West included the
whole series stretched in a rough gradation from the
definitely established region where people had achieved
satisfaction with their mode of life, out to the spaces
known only by the reports of transient visitors.

The explorers and hunters and traders did not pin
down and hold a line of advancing civilization; they
merely passed through the region and came back to
tell their story. They belonged to the West, however,

and their part was important because it brought to the edge of settlement and to the East two things: a lure that induced further movement of the frontier, and a knowledge of paths and conditions to guide such advance. The waves of progress that followed the frontier—material development and cultural and aesthetic achievements—are more like the westward march of the frontier. It is probably more sound, however, to regard them as the gradual reassertion of basic elements of civilization inhibited by hardships and the demands of the frontier and emerging in modified forms when those demands are lightened.

The West everywhere presented (1) relatively unfettered political and social conditions, and (2) powerful forces to be overcome. Into it came people with well-defined ideas of life. The result was that original ideals and mores were modified both by the freedom and by the resistant nature of the primitive environment. At first the West forced the pioneer to put a portion of his civilization aside. Wisely he adjusted himself to the situation. But as rapidly as possible he introduced what he had held in abeyance, and always with alterations due to his new surroundings and experiences. This modified culture in turn affected the East, and its leaven continually helped to make the whole people different from the older East of Europe.

The West has been so comprehensive, however, that despite this persistent tendency it has never been homogeneous. It has always included varying conditions and people of different aims. The purposes of the trader and settler were antithetical. The squatter and the land speculator were natural enemies. In the North and the South, in the wooded trans-Allegheny and on the western plains the frontier itself showed widely divergent aspects. The Western war hawks of 1812 were a coalition, as were the expansionists of 1844. Jefferson Davis' state of Mississippi in the 1850's was as much a part of the West as Lincoln's Illinois. And different elements joined in the western protests between 1872 and 1912.

That the West was constantly changing is obvious. The first West was not easily distinguishable from the seacoast settlements. The piedmont West and the transmontane West were progressively different stages. The colonial West as a whole was made up of individual and largely unrelated elements, affecting the East in local issues such as that of Nathaniel Bacon in Virginia, the Paxton Boys in Pennsylvania, and the Regulators in North Carolina. But one cannot fail to notice the prevalent outcropping of a democratic spirit.

After the Revolution the West centered in the trans-Allegheny region, with the far side of the Mississippi calling to such souls as Thomas Jefferson and Philip Nolan, and the people of the cis-Allegheny West trying to level the obstacles that lay between the Atlantic and the Ohio. Western democracy became intensified and contributed largely to Jefferson's victory. Separatism was rampant beyond the mountains in this period; nevertheless, nationalism sprang from the very existence of the West as a common possession of the diversely minded states. Unity was further advanced by treaties favorable to the West with England and Spain and by the acquisition of statehood in Kentucky and Tennessee and in Ohio—first fruit of an ordinance representing old institutions changed to suit new conditions.

With the purchase of Louisiana and the subsequent crumbling of foreign competition from St. Augustine to Puget Sound, the West assumed heroic proportions. It called to fur companies, farmers, and miners. Migration became a tide, and with numbers came power. Nationalistic spirit was more clearly a possession of the West with the greater participation of westerners in national politics, and because of the rapidity of expansion which fostered and was fostered by the idea of manifest destiny. Southerners went westward with cotton, and northerners with grain. In the end the West gave with unequal generosity to the two sides, and, having prolonged the existence of slavery by its early promises, had a great part in its destruction.

After the middle of the nineteenth century, with national territorial limits practically determined, the emphasis changed from expansion to utilization. The frontier still existed—a vital westward-moving zone— and following it came the transforming ideas of more settled life, reasserting the old but partaking of the new. The West still contained a reservoir of resources and free land, giving opportunity and mobility to the speculator and to the man without funds. This had tended to postpone monopoly and tight class struggle. But now the inevitable industrial advance brought economic unrest and typical Middle Western reactions, possibly accentuated by a realization that the Far Western offer of mobility was decreasingly effective. In 1890 the Superintendent of the Census announced that the frontier was gone, whereupon Turner began interpretative writings which form the soundest basis of our study of the frontier and the West.

The West, however, did not disappear with the frontier. Each decade has shown the persistence of the westward movement of people. Certain improvident accompaniments of the process of subjugation have made the West a region of new problems which will have to be solved. The absence of a frontier and free land, and the development of a new industrial order, have changed the dominant aspect of our national life. But the earlier transforming forces have not been erased. Since 1890 the marked characteristic has been the establishment of the comforts and refinements of life. The motivating spirit has been discontent, and the continuing virile effect of the West is shown in various modified forms of education, literature, and the arts. When satisfaction with a mode of life shall have crossed the country, permeating every part, the distinction between East and West will be gone; but as long as there is a region of incomplete development where a younger spirit and fresher and more open conditions are changing old ideas into new forms, there will still be the West.